Smoking
Bans

Smoking Bans

David L. Hudson, Jr.

SERIES CONSULTING EDITOR
Alan Marzilli, M.A., J.D.

CHELSEA HOUSE
PUBLISHERS

A Haights Cross Communications Company

Philadelphia

CHELSEA HOUSE PUBLISHERS

VP, New Product Development   Sally Cheney
Director of Production   Kim Shinners
Creative Manager   Takeshi Takahashi
Manufacturing Manager   Diann Grasse

Staff for SMOKING BANS

Executive Editor   Lee Marcott
Senior Editor   Tara Koellhoffer
Production Editor   Megan Emery
Assistant Photo Editor   Noelle Nardone
Series and Cover Designer   Keith Trego
Layout   21st Century Publishing and Communications, Inc.

A Haights Cross Communications ✦ Company

http://www.chelseahouse.com

First Printing

1 3 5 7 9 8 6 4 2

Library of Congress Cataloging-in-Publication Data

Hudson, David (David L.), 1969-
  Smoking bans / by David L. Hudson, Jr.
    p. cm. — (Point/counterpoint)
  Includes bibliographical references and index.
  ISBN 0-7910-7974-0
  1. Smoking—United States—Juvenile literature. 2. Smoking—Law and
legislation—United States—Juvenile literature. 3. Tobacco industry—United
States—Juvenile literature. I. Title. II. Point-counterpoint (Philadelphia, Pa.)
  HV5760.H83 2004
  362.29'6'0973—dc22
                                                        2004000312

||||||| CONTENTS

Introduction
Alan Marzilli, M.A., J.D.
Durham, North Carolina

The debates presented in POINT/COUNTERPOINT are among the most interesting and controversial in contemporary American society, but studying them is more than an academic activity. They affect every citizen; they are the issues that today's leaders debate and tomorrow's will decide. The reader may one day play a central role in resolving them.

Why study both sides of the debate? It's possible that the reader will not yet have formed any opinion at all on the subject of this volume—but this is unlikely. It is more likely that the reader will already hold an opinion, probably a strong one, and very probably one formed without full exposure to the arguments of the other side. It is rare to hear an argument presented in a balanced way, and it is easy to form an opinion on too little information; these books will help to fill in the informational gaps that can never be avoided. More important, though, is the practical function of the series: Skillful argumentation requires a thorough knowledge of *both* sides—though there are seldom only two, and only by knowing what an opponent is likely to assert can one form an articulate response.

Perhaps more important is that listening to the other side sometimes helps one to see an opponent's arguments in a more human way. For example, Sister Helen Prejean, one of the nation's most visible opponents of capital punishment, has been deeply affected by her interactions with the families of murder victims. Seeing the families' grief and pain, she understands much better why people support the death penalty, and she is able to carry out her advocacy with a greater sensitivity to the needs and beliefs of those who do not agree with her. Her relativism, in turn, lends credibility to her work. Dismissing the other side of the argument as totally without merit can be too easy—it is far more useful to understand the nature of the controversy and the reasons *why* the issue defies resolution.

The most controversial issues of all are often those that center on a constitutional right. The Bill of Rights—the first ten amendments to the U.S. Constitution—spells out some of the most fundamental rights that distinguish the governmental system of the United States from those that allow fewer (or other) freedoms. But the sparsely worded document is open to interpretation, and clauses of only a few words are often at the heart of national debates. The Bill of Rights was meant to protect individual liberties; but the needs of some individuals clash with those of society as a whole, and when this happens someone has to decide where to draw the line. Thus the Constitution becomes a battleground between the rights of individuals to do as they please and the responsibility of the government to protect its citizens. The First Amendment's guarantee of "freedom of speech," for example, leads to a number of difficult questions. Some forms of expression, such as burning an American flag, lead to public outrage—but nevertheless are said to be protected by the First Amendment. Other types of expression that most people find objectionable, such as sexually explicit material involving children, are not protected because they are considered harmful. The question is not only where to draw the line, but how to do this without infringing on the personal liberties on which the United States was built.

The Bill of Rights raises many other questions about individual rights and the societal "good." Is a prayer before a high school football game an "establishment of religion" prohibited by the First Amendment? Does the Second Amendment's promise of "the right to bear arms" include concealed handguns? Is stopping and frisking someone standing on a corner known to be frequented by drug dealers a form of "unreasonable search and seizure" in violation of the Fourth Amendment? Although the nine-member U.S. Supreme Court has the ultimate authority in interpreting the Constitution, its answers do not always satisfy the public. When a group of nine people—sometimes by a five-to-four vote—makes a decision that affects the lives of hundreds of millions, public outcry can be expected. And the composition of the Court does change over time, so even a landmark decision is not guaranteed to stand forever. The limits of constitutional protection are always in flux.

These issues make headlines, divide courts, and decide elections. They are the questions most worthy of national debate, and this series aims to cover them as thoroughly as possible. Each volume sets out some of the key arguments surrounding a particular issue, even some views that most people consider extreme or radical—but presents a balanced perspective on the issue. Excerpts from the relevant laws and judicial opinions and references to central concepts, source material, and advocacy groups help the reader to explore the issues even further and to read "the letter of the law" just as the legislatures and the courts have established it.

It may seem that some debates—such as those over capital punishment and abortion, debates with a strong moral component— will never be resolved. But American history offers numerous examples of controversies that once seemed insurmountable but now are effectively settled, even if only on the surface. Abolitionists met with widespread resistance to their efforts to end slavery, and the controversy over that issue threatened to cleave the nation in two; but today public debate over the merits of slavery would be unthinkable, though racial inequalities still plague the nation. Similarly unthinkable at one time was suffrage for women and minorities, but this is now a matter of course. Distributing information about contraception once was a crime. Societies change, and attitudes change, and new questions of social justice are raised constantly while the old ones fade into irrelevancy.

Whatever the root of the controversy, the books in POINT/ COUNTERPOINT seek to explain to the reader the origins of the debate, the current state of the law, and the arguments on both sides. The goal of the series is to inform the reader about the issues facing not only American politicians, but all of the nation's citizens, and to encourage the reader to become more actively involved in resolving these debates, as a voter, a concerned citizen, a journalist, an activist, or an elected official. Democracy is based on education, and every voice counts—so every opinion must be an informed one.

———————•———————•———————•———————

The harmful effects of tobacco are well documented, and the numbers of smokers have declined since the mid-twentieth century, when over half of Americans smoked. Despite the evidence, many Americans continue to light up, even though it is becoming more difficult to find places to do so. Once allowed in airplanes, movie theaters, office buildings, grocery stores, and even college class-rooms, smoking is now banned from many public places. However, smokers have begun to fight back against the increasing number of local laws banning smoking from *all* public places, even bars and restaurants. They say that such sweeping bans infringe on freedom of choice, but the bans' supporters say that clean air is essential to preserve the health of nonsmokers. This volume examines the backlash against smoking and the tobacco industry, including class-action lawsuits by people who have suffered from smoking-related illnesses, and limitations on tobacco advertising. To many people, such measures are needed to protect the public from a dangerous industry, but critics say that people should be allowed to make their own choices, good or bad.

History of Tobacco and Its Regulation

Tobacco has been a staple in American society since its introduction more than four hundred years ago. It became a leading crop of many early American colonies and continued to drive the economy of those colonies as they entered statehood. Even today, it remains a major force as tobacco companies gross billions of dollars each year. Millions of Americans and people worldwide regularly use cigarettes, cigars, and other tobacco products. However, tobacco also has long been a burning controversy in society. It is, in the words of the U.S. Department of Justice, "the single leading cause of preventable death in the United States." [1]

Most early attacks against tobacco were based on moral grounds. Currently, the objection to tobacco centers primarily on medical reasons. For years, many people have railed against tobacco. As early as 1604, British King James I attacked tobacco in his treatise *A Counter-Blaste to Tobacco*. He described tobacco smoking as "a custom loathsome to the eye, hateful to the nose, harmful to the brain, dangerous to the lung, and the black stinking fume thereof, nearest resembling the horribly Stygian smoke of the pit that is bottomless."[2]

By the end of the seventeenth century, leading practitioners of medicine in Paris began to suspect that tobacco was harmful

Smoking and Religion

Although some traditional religions have been known to use smoking as part of ritual, no modern religion actively encourages the use of tobacco by members. In fact, many faiths forbid tobacco entirely.

During the month of fasting of Ramadan, Muslims are required to give up smoking—including passive, or secondhand, smoking.

Several branches of Christianity forbid smoking by adherents, including:

- American Society of Friends (Quakers)

- Methodist Church

- Baptists

- Mormons (Church of Jesus Christ of Latter-day Saints)

- The Salvation Army

- Seventh-Day Adventists

Hinduism, too, discourages smoking. According to Hindu religious leader Swami Amarananda of the Hindu Centre of Geneva, "Tobacco is traditionally seen as a *vyasana* or an unhealthy dependence. And the goal of spiritual life lies in the cessation of suffering, access to bliss and freedom from the bondage of nature. So a *vyasana* matches ill with a spiritual life."*

Source: *http://hinduism.about.com/library/weekly/aa052900a.htm*.

to humans. In 1853, physician L. B. Coles called tobacco "a deadly narcotic" in his book *The Beauties and Deformities of Tobacco-Using*.[3] Such views were in the minority, though. Most of those opposed to tobacco criticized smoking on moral grounds, not for health reasons. Furthermore, most members of the medical community and the general public viewed smoking as something that could be done in moderation.

At the end of the nineteenth century, only one in a hundred Americans smoked tobacco. Around that time, several states, including Iowa, Tennessee, and North Dakota, outlawed the sale of cigarettes. A suit was filed to challenge the Tennessee law. Specifically, the case concerned a Tennessee law that outlawed the selling or giving away of "cigarettes, cigarette paper or substitute for the same." The penalty was a $50 fine. In 1900, the U.S. Supreme Court ruled in *Austin* v. *Tennessee* that the state could lawfully ban the product because of its (the state's) general power to protect public heath and welfare.[4]

> • **Could a state ban the sale of cigarettes within its borders? Should states make smoking illegal?**

Even though the Court would not demonize tobacco as an inherently harmful product, it recognized that the Tennessee law was "designed for the protection of the public health."[5] The defendant, William B. Austin, had purchased large quantities of cigarettes from the American Tobacco Company in Durham, North Carolina, and then sold them in Tennessee. He argued that the state law violated the commerce clause of the U.S. Constitution. The commerce clause provides that Congress—and only Congress—has the power to regulate commerce between the states, called interstate commerce. Tennessee argued that it had the right under its general police power to protect the health of its citizenry. The U.S. Supreme Court sided with the state of Tennessee, writing that it could not "force into the markets of a state, against its will, articles or commodities which, like cigarettes, may not unreasonably be held to be injurious to health."[6]

In 1920, the Eighteenth Amendment, which provided for the start of Prohibition, went into effect. The amendment prohibited the sale and distribution of alcohol. Tobacco industry executives feared their product would be next. Government officials did not ban cigarettes, however. Instead, they found another use for them—they taxed them. In 1921, Iowa became the first state to tax cigarettes.[7]

Although efforts were made to enforce the ban on alcoholic beverages, many people found ways to buy and sell liquor illegally. It eventually became clear that Prohibition was not

(continued on page 17)

FROM THE BENCH

Austin v. *Tennessee*, 179 U.S. 343 (1900)

From the first settlement of the colony of Virginia to the present day tobacco has been one of the most profitable and important products of agriculture and commerce, and while its effects may be injurious to some, its extensive use over practically the entire globe is a remarkable tribute to its popularity and value. We are clearly of opinion that it cannot be classed with diseased cattle or meats, decayed fruit, or other articles, the use of which is a menace to the health of the entire community. Congress, too, has recognized tobacco in its various forms as a legitimate article of commerce by requiring licenses to be taken for its manufacture and sale, imposing a revenue tax upon each package of cigarettes put upon the market, and by making express regulations for their manufacture and sale, their exportation and importation. Cigarettes are but one of the numerous manufactures of tobacco, and we cannot take judicial notice of the fact that it is more noxious in this form than in any other. Whatever might be our individual views as to its deleterious tendencies, we cannot hold that any article which Congress recognizes in so many ways is not a legitimate article of commerce....

It was held ... in *Powell* v. *Pennsylvania, 127 U.S. 678* , 32 L. ed. 253, 8 Sup. Ct. Rep. 992, 1257, that a statute of Pennsylvania prohibiting the manufacture or sale of oleomargarine was a lawful exercise by the state of its power to protect by police regulations the public health, and that it neither denied to persons within the jurisdiction of the state the equal protection of the laws, nor deprived them of their property without compensation, and was not otherwise repugnant to the 14th Amendment. Said Mr. Justice Harlan: "It [this court] cannot adjudge that the defendant's rights of liberty and property, as thus defined, have been infringed by the statute of Pennsylvania, without holding that, although it may have been enacted in good faith for the objects expressed in its title, namely, to protect the public health and to prevent the adulteration of dairy products and fraud in the sale thereof, it has, in fact, no real or substantial relation to those objects. The court is unable to affirm that this legislation has no real or substantial relation to such objects." So, too, in *Plumley* v. *Massachusetts, 155 U.S. 461* , 39 L. ed. 223, 5 Inters. Com. Rep. 590, 15 Sup. Ct. Rep. 154, a statute of Massachusetts prohibiting the sale of oleomargarine artificially colored so as to cause it to look like yellow butter, and so brought into the state, was decided not to be in conflict with the commerce clause of the Constitution. These cases recognize the fact that intoxicating liquors belong to a class of commodities which, in the opinion of a great many estimable people, are deleterious in their effects, demoralizing in their tendencies, and often fatal in their excessive indulgence; and that, while their employment as a medicine may sometimes be beneficial, their habitual and constant use as a beverage, whatever it may be to individuals, is injurious to the community. It may be that their evil effects have been exaggerated, and that, though their use is usually attended with more or less danger, it is by no means open to universal condemnation. It is, however, within the power of each state to investigate the subject and to determine its policy in that particular. If the legislative body come deliberately to the conclusion that a due regard for the public safety and morals requires a suppression of the liquor traffic, there is nothing in the commercial clause of the Constitution, or in the 14th Amendment to that instrument, to forbid its doing so. While, perhaps, it may not wholly prohibit the use or sale of them for medicinal purposes, it may hedge about their use as a general beverage such restrictions as it pleases. Nor can we deny to the legislature the power to impose restrictions upon the sale of noxious or poisonous drugs, such as opium and other similar articles, extremely valuable as medicines, but equally baneful to the habitual user.

Cigarettes do not seem until recently to have attracted the attention of the public as more injurious than other forms of tobacco; nor are we now prepared to take judicial notice of any special injury resulting from their use or to indorse the opinion of the supreme court of Tennessee that "they are inherently bad and bad only." At the same time we should be shutting our eyes to what is constantly passing before them were we to affect an ignorance of the fact that a belief in their deleterious effects, particularly upon young people, has become very general, and that communications are constantly finding their way into the public press denouncing their use as fraught with great danger to the youth of both sexes. Without undertaking to affirm or deny their evil effects, we think it within the province of the legislature to say how far they may be sold, or to prohibit their sale entirely, after they have been taken from the original packages or have left the hands of the importer, provided no discrimination be used as against such as are imported from other states, and there be no reason to doubt that the act in question is designed for the protection of the public health.

We have had repeated occasion to hold, where state legislation has been attacked as violative either of the power of Congress over interstate commerce, or of the 14th Amendment to the Constitution, that, if the action of the state legislature were as a bona fide exercise of its police power, and dictated by a genuine regard for the preservation of the public health or safety, such legislation would be respected, though it might interfere indirectly with interstate commerce....

We are therefore of opinion that although the state of Tennessee may not wholly interdict commerce in cigarettes it is not, in the language of Chief Justice Taney in *The License Cases*, "bound to furnish a market for it [them], nor to abstain from the passage of any law which it may deem necessary or advisable to guard the health or morals of its citizens, although such law may discourage importation, or diminish the profits of the importer, or lessen the revenue of the general government."...

Most pertinent to this case, and, as we think, covering its principle completely, is the opinion of this court in *May* v. *New Orleans*, 178 U.S. 496 , 44 L. ed. 1165, 20 Sup. Ct. Rep. 976. . . . This involved the validity of certain tax assessments made by the city of New Orleans upon the merchandise and stock in trade of the plaintiff, which consisted of dry goods imported from foreign countries, upon which duties had been levied by and paid to the general government. The goods were put up and sold in packages, a large number of such packages being inclosed in wooden cases or boxes for the purposes of importation. Upon arrival at New Orleans the boxes were opened, the packages taken out and sold unbroken. The question was whether the box or case containing these packages, or the packages themselves were the original packages within the case of *Brown* v. *Maryland*, 12 Wheat. 419, 6 L. ed. 678. It was conceded that, so long as the packages remained in their original cases, they were not subject to taxation, but the court held that this immunity ceased as soon as the boxes were opened....

The real question in this case is whether the size of the package in which the importation is actually made is to govern; or, the size of the package in which bona fide transactions are carried on between the manufacturer and the wholesale dealer residing in different states. We hold to the latter view. The whole theory of the exemption of the original package from the operation of state laws is based upon the idea that the property is imported in the ordinary form in which, from time immemorial, foreign goods have been brought into the country. These have gone at once into the hands of the wholesale dealers, who have been in the habit of breaking the packages and distributing their contents among the several retail dealers throughout the state. It was with reference to this method of doing business that the doctrine of the exemption of the original package grew up. But taking the words "original package" in their literal sense, a number of so-called original package manufactories have been started through the country, whose business it is to manufacture goods for the express purpose of sending their products into other states in minute packages, that may at once go into the hands of the retail dealers and consumers, and thus bid defiance to the laws of the state against their importation and sale.... This court has repeatedly held that, so far from lending its authority to frauds upon the sanitary laws of the several states, we are bound to respect such laws and to aid in their enforcement, so far as can be done without infringing upon the constitutional rights of the parties. The consequences of our adoption of defendant's contention would be far reaching and disastrous....

The question is not in what packages the law requires the cigarettes to be packed for the purpose of taxation, but, what are the packages in which they are usually transported from one state to another where the transaction is bona fide and for the legitimate purposes of trade and commerce?

We are satisfied the conclusion of the Supreme Court of Tennessee was correct, and it is therefore affirmed.

(continued from page 13)

working. The Eighteenth Amendment was repealed with the Twenty-first Amendment, which took effect in 1933. The era of Prohibition was over.

> • **Do you think tobacco could ever be banned like alcohol was in the early part of the twentieth century?**

In the twentieth century, the medical community began to realize more and more the dangers of smoking. In 1939, Franz Hermann Muller of the University of Cologne's Pathological Institute in Germany observed that the increase in smoking after World War I "runs parallel with the increase in primary lung cancer."[8]

Despite such findings, however, tobacco became immensely popular. By 1950, 50 percent of American adults smoked tobacco.[9] World War II had led to an increase in smoking. Author and journalist Richard Kluger writes that "the cultural habituation of Americans to their cigarettes was seductively advanced by Hollywood."[10]

In the 1940s and 1950s, the Federal Trade Commission (FTC) began to police the tobacco companies for their advertisements that cigarettes were harmless. By the end of 1953, the American Medical Association (AMA) stopped accepting cigarette ads in its leading scientific journal, *Journal of the American Medical Association.* That same year, Dr. Ernst Wynder published a study in the magazine *Cancer Research.* His study examined the effects of tobacco exposure on mice. He painted a group of mice with tobacco smoke. Twenty months later, only 10 percent of the painted animals were still alive, while 58 percent of the mice that were unpainted survived. "On many fronts and in many laboratories, the case against smoking grew in the late fifties," writes Kluger.[11]

The tobacco companies were worried about these medical studies. They enlisted the services of a leading public relations firm and formed the Tobacco Industry Research Committee.

The tobacco companies engaged in a concentrated process of research and public relations. Still, for every dollar spent on research, tobacco companies spent $200 on the advertisement and promotion of their products.[12]

The tobacco companies managed to convince many members of the public that smoking really wasn't that bad. In 1964, a leading tobacco executive told the *New York Times*: "I don't believe the present product will prove to be health hazard." At the same time, a few people involved in research for the tobacco companies recognized the dangers. A 1961 memo drafted by a scientist for Philip Morris stated: "A morally acceptable low-carcinogen cigarette may be possible. Its development will require TIME, MONEY and UNFAILING DETERMINATION."[13]

The Surgeon General's Advisory Committee on Smoking and Health conducted its first meeting in November 1962. The committee ended up issuing a 387-page report. It concluded that "Cigarette smoking is a health hazard of sufficient importance in the United States to warrant appropriate remedial action."[14]

"As the scientific evidence against it gathered throughout the 1950s, the tobacco industry did not merely deny, dispute, and mock it as a defensive strategy; it also spent heavily on advertising as its prime offensive weapon to convince its customers that the product was well worth any risk that might accompany their use of it," Kluger wrote.[15]

In the 1960s, however, the public began to realize the harms of smoking. A 1968 Gallup poll reported that 71 percent of the public believed that smoking caused cancer. Just ten years before, only 44 percent believed it did.

Gradually, a consensus grew within the medical and scientific community that smoking had deleterious effects upon public health. This led to increased calls for bans on smoking in public places. Many states began to pass so-called

(continued on page 22)

FROM THE BENCH

FDA v. BROWN & WILLIAMSON TOBACCO CORPORATION, 592 U.S. 120 (2000)

March 21, 2000

This case involves one of the most troubling public health problems facing our Nation today: the thousands of premature deaths that occur each year because of tobacco use. In 1996, the Food and Drug Administration (FDA), after having expressly disavowed any such authority since its inception, asserted jurisdiction to regulate tobacco products. . . . The FDA concluded that nicotine is a "drug" within the meaning of the Food, Drug, and Cosmetic Act (FDCA or Act), . . . and that cigarettes and smokeless tobacco are "combination products" that deliver nicotine to the body. . . . Pursuant to this authority, it promulgated regulations intended to reduce tobacco consumption among children and adolescents. . . . The agency believed that, because most tobacco consumers begin their use before reaching the age of 18, curbing tobacco use by minors could substantially reduce the prevalence of addiction in future generations and thus the incidence of tobacco-related death and disease. . . .

Regardless of how serious the problem an administrative agency seeks to address, however, it may not exercise its authority "in a manner that is inconsistent with the administrative structure that Congress enacted into law." . . . And although agencies are generally entitled to deference in the interpretation of statutes that they administer, a reviewing "court, as well as the agency, must give effect to the unambiguously expressed intent of Congress." . . . In this case, we believe that Congress has clearly precluded the FDA from asserting jurisdiction to regulate tobacco products. Such authority is inconsistent with the intent that Congress has expressed in the FDCA's overall regulatory scheme and in the tobacco-specific legislation that it has enacted subsequent to the FDCA. In light of this clear intent, the FDA's assertion of jurisdiction is impermissible. . . .

The FDA promulgated these regulations pursuant to its authority to regulate "restricted devices." . . . using the Act's drug authorities, device authorities, or both, depending on "how the public health goals of the act can be best accomplished." ... Given the greater flexibility in the FDCA for the regulation of devices, the FDA determined that "the device authorities provide the most appropriate basis for regulating cigarettes and smokeless tobacco." ... Under *21 U.S.C. 360j*(e), the agency may "require that a device be restricted to sale, distribution, or use ... upon such other conditions as [the FDA] may prescribe in such regulation, if, because of its potentiality for harmful effect or the collateral measures necessary to its use, [the FDA] determines that there cannot otherwise be reasonable assurance of its safety and effectiveness." The FDA reasoned that its regulations fell within the authority granted by §360j(e) because they related to the sale or distribution of tobacco products and were necessary for providing a reasonable assurance of safety. ...

Respondents, a group of tobacco manufacturers, retailers, and advertisers, filed suit in United States District Court for the Middle District of North Carolina challenging the regulations. ... They moved for summary judgment on the grounds that the FDA lacked jurisdiction to regulate tobacco products as customarily marketed, the regulations exceeded the FDA's authority under *21 U.S.C. 360j*(e), and the advertising restrictions violated the First Amendment. ... The court held that the FDCA authorizes the FDA to regulate tobacco products as customarily marketed and that the FDA's access and labeling regulations are permissible, but it also found that the agency's advertising and promotion restrictions exceed its authority under §360j(e). ... The court stayed implementation of the regulations it found valid (except the prohibition on the sale of tobacco products to minors) and certified its order for immediate interlocutory appeal. ...

The Court of Appeals for the Fourth Circuit reversed, holding that Congress has not granted the FDA jurisdiction to regulate tobacco products. ... Examining the FDCA as a whole, the court concluded that the FDA's regulation of tobacco products would create a number of internal inconsistencies. ... Various provisions of the Act require the agency to determine that any regulated product is "safe" before it can be sold or allowed to remain on the market, yet the FDA found in its rulemaking proceeding that tobacco products are "dangerous" and "unsafe." Thus, the FDA would apparently have to ban tobacco products, a result the court found clearly contrary to congressional intent. This apparent anomaly, the Court of Appeals concluded, demonstrates that Congress did not intend to give the FDA authority to regulate tobacco. The court also found that evidence external to the FDCA confirms this conclusion. Importantly, the FDA consistently stated before 1995 that it lacked jurisdiction over tobacco, and Congress has enacted several tobacco-specific statutes fully cognizant of the FDA's position. In fact, the court reasoned, Congress has considered and rejected many bills that would have given the agency such authority. This, along with the absence of any intent by the enacting Congress in 1938 to subject tobacco products to regulation under the FDCA, demonstrates that Congress intended to withhold such authority from the FDA. Having resolved the jurisdictional question against the agency, the Court of Appeals did not address whether the regulations exceed the FDA's authority under *21 U.S.C. 360j*(e) or violate the First Amendment. . . .

A threshold issue is the appropriate framework for analyzing the FDA's assertion of authority to regulate tobacco products. Because this case involves an administrative agency's construction of a statute that it administers . . . a reviewing court must first ask "whether Congress has directly spoken to the precise question at issue." If Congress has done so, the inquiry is at an end; the court "must give effect to the unambiguously expressed intent of Congress." . . . But if Congress has not specifically addressed the question, a reviewing court must respect the agency's construction of the statute so long as it is permissible. . . .

With these principles in mind, we find that Congress has directly spoken to the issue here and precluded the FDA's jurisdiction to regulate tobacco products.

. . . [I]t is clear that Congress intended to exclude tobacco products from the FDA's jurisdiction.

By no means do we question the seriousness of the problem that the FDA has sought to address. The agency has amply demonstrated that tobacco use, particularly among children and adolescents, poses perhaps the single most significant threat to public health in the United States. Nonetheless, no matter how "important, conspicuous, and controversial" the issue, and regardless of how likely the public is to hold the Executive Branch politically accountable, *post*, at 31, an administrative agency's power to regulate in the public interest must always be grounded in a valid grant of authority from Congress. . . .

(continued from page 18)

clean indoor air acts. To this day, litigation continues as more and more states and municipalities impose smoking bans, even in places traditionally associated with smoking, such as bars and taverns.

The public health findings on smoking led to increasing numbers of lawsuits against the tobacco industry. First individuals, then classes of individuals and even state attorneys general began to file suit against tobacco companies, accusing them of fraud and deceit in marketing an addictive product while concealing just how addictive and harmful their products are.

"No one could seriously dispute that today smoking is a social and political issue of enormous intensity and import," wrote law professor Martin Redish. "The smoking controversy involves a variety of heavily contested issues, implicating questions of scientific theory, individual free choice, social responsibility, and the scope of governmental power."[16]

Smoking remains a burning issue. Looming questions remain regarding the constitutionality of smoking bans, product liability suits against tobacco companies, and whether it is constitutional to restrict tobacco advertising. Another looming issue concerns the large amount of donations made to political candidates by the tobacco industry. Anti-smoking advocates recently released a study showing that tobacco interests spent more than $20 million in 2002 to lobby political leaders.[17]

Still another major issue involving smoking concerns the Food and Drug Administration (FDA) and its failed attempts to regulate tobacco. The U.S. Supreme Court ruled in 2000 that the FDA did not have the authority to regulate tobacco as a drug in *FDA* v. *Brown & Williamson Tobacco Corp.*[18] However, measures have been introduced in Congress to give the FDA the necessary authority to regulate tobacco.

This book examines three major controversies that involve smoking, including: (1) smoking bans; (2) tort lawsuits filed against tobacco companies for injuries suffered by smokers and those harmed by secondhand smoke; and (3) restrictions on tobacco advertising.

Smoking Bans Protect Public Health

Gail Routh worked as a flight attendant for twenty-seven years, beginning in 1972. A nonsmoker all her life, Routh nonetheless contracted lung cancer after working in close contact with secondhand smoke on airplanes in the years before smoking was banned on airline flights. Routh sued Philip Morris USA, R.J. Reynolds Tobacco Co., Lorillard Tobacco, and Brown & Williamson Tobacco Corporation, claiming that the exposure to secondhand smoke had caused both her lung cancer and conditions of chronic sinusitis and bronchitis.

In a verdict that surprised many observers, in October 2003, a jury in Florida decided against Routh. Although the jury declared that secondhand smoke could be a cause of cancer, it could not be proven conclusively that it had been the cause of Routh's own medical condition.

The lawyer who represented Routh in the case said, "This is a woman who was healthy as could be when she started working in 1972, a lifetime nonsmoker who had no medical problems. Everything points to secondhand smoke as the cause." [1]

Smokers often insist they have the individual right to smoke. Smoking, after all, is still a legal activity for adults. However, nonsmokers have rights, too. The personal preferences of smokers should not trump the right of nonsmokers to breathe clean air in a healthy environment. In other words, smokers may have the right to harm their own health but not the health of others.

The clear trend in American society is to segregate, if not eliminate, smoking in public places. Smoking is prohibited in airplanes, sports stadiums, places of employment, and many restaurants. Nonsmokers have successfully petitioned city and state legislators for an increasing array of smoking restrictions. Many state and local governments have responded with broad restrictions on smokers. The state of Delaware passed a law prohibiting smoking in "any indoor enclosed area to which the general public is invited or in which the general public is permitted." [2] New York City and Dallas are two examples of cities that have recently passed highly restrictive smoking laws. Commentators estimated in a 2002 article that more than 1,400 local jurisdictions across the United States have passed antismoking regulations. [3]

• **Does your state or city have a smoking ban? If not, would you support such a ban?**

Scientific evidence confirms that smoking—including secondhand smoke—is harmful.

In 1964, the U.S. Surgeon General declared that smoking was a health hazard and causally related to lung cancer. The next year, the U.S. Congress passed the Cigarette Labeling and Advertising Act, which required cigarette manufacturers to include warning labels on all cigarette advertisements. The mandated warning read: "Caution: cigarette smoking may be hazardous to your health." [4] In 1970, Congress amended the law in the Public

1986 Surgeon General Report—The Health Consequences of Involuntary Smoking

From the Foreword by Assistant Secretary for Health Robert E. Windom, M.D.:

The data reviewed in 17 previous U.S. Public Health Service reports on the health consequences of smoking have conclusively established cigarette smoking as the largest single preventable cause of premature death and disability in the United States.

The question whether tobacco smoke is harmful to smokers was answered more than 20 years ago. As a result, many scientists began to question whether the low levels of exposure to environmental tobacco smoke (ETS) received by nonsmokers could also be harmful.

The current Report, The Health Consequences of Involuntary Smoking, examines the evidence that even the lower exposure to smoke received by the nonsmoker carries with it a health risk. Use of the term "involuntary smoking" denotes that for many nonsmokers, exposure to ETS is the result of an unavoidable consequence of being in proximity to smokers. It is the first Report in the health consequences of smoking series to establish a health risk due to tobacco smoke exposure for individuals other than the smoker, and represents the work of more than 60 distinguished physicians and scientists, both in this country and abroad.

After careful examination of the available evidence, the following overall conclusions can be reached:

(1) Involuntary smoking is a cause of disease, including lung cancer in healthy nonsmokers.

(2) The children of parents who smoke compared with the children of non-smoking parents have an increased frequency of respiratory infections, increased respiratory symptoms, and slightly smaller rates of increase in lung function as the lung matures.

Health Cigarette Smoking Act to require an even stricter message: "Warning: The Surgeon General Has Determined That Cigarette Smoking Is Dangerous To Your Health."[5]

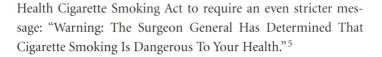

(3) The simple separation of smokers and nonsmokers within the same air space may reduce, but does not eliminate, the exposure of nonsmokers to environmental tobacco smoke.

Exposure to environmental tobacco smoke occurs at home, at the worksite, in public, and in other places where smoking is permitted. The quality of the indoor environment must be a concern of all who control and occupy that environment. Protection of individuals from exposure to environmental tobacco smoke is therefore a responsibility shared by all:

- As parents and adults we must protect the health of our children by not exposing them to environmental tobacco smoke.

- As employers and employees we must ensure that the act of smoking does not expose the nonsmoker to tobacco smoke.

- For smokers, it is their responsibility to assure that their behavior does not jeopardize the health of others.

- For nonsmokers, it is their responsibility to provide a supportive environment for smokers who are attempting to stop.

Actions taken by individuals, employers, and employee organizations reflect the growing concern for protecting nonsmokers. The number of laws and regulations enacted at the national, State, and local level governing smoking in public has increased substantially over the past 10 years, and surveys conducted by numerous organizations show strong public support for these actions among both smokers and nonsmokers.

As a Nation, we have made substantial progress in addressing the enormous toll inflicted by active smoking. Efforts to improve and protect individual health must be not only continued but strengthened. On the basis of the evidence presented in this Report, it is clear that actions to protect nonsmokers from ETS exposure not only are warranted but are essential to protect public health.

Source: *The Health Consequences of Involuntary Smoking: A Report of the Surgeon General*, Rockville, MD: U.S. Department of Health and Human Services, 1986.

In 1986, the U.S. Surgeon General declared that even involuntary smoking was harmful. Environmental tobacco smoke (ETS), also called secondhand smoke, consists of sidestream smoke and mainstream smoke. Sidestream smoke is the smoke emitted from the tip of a burning cigarette. Mainstream smoke is the smoke exhaled by the smoker.

In 1993, a report by the Environmental Protection Agency concluded: "Based on the weight of the available scientific evidence, the U.S. Environmental Protection Agency (EPA) has concluded that the widespread exposure to ETS in the United States presents a serious and substantial public health impact."[6] The report added that for adults, "ETS is a human lung carcinogen, responsible for approximately 3,000 lung cancer deaths annually in U.S. nonsmokers."[7] The National Cancer Institute reported that there are many harmful effects associated with ETS, including: "acute lower respiratory tract infections in children, asthma induction and exacerbation in children, eye and nasal irritation in adults and lung cancer."[8] In sum, there is no doubt that smoking affects more than just the health of smokers. Non-smokers who are exposed to smoking can suffer harm as well. For this reason alone, smoking bans serve the public interest in the health, safety, and welfare of nonsmokers and children.

Smoking bans in the workplace are justified.

Smoking bans in the workplace are essential for the health and well-being of employees. Employers have a common law duty to provide a safe and healthy working environment for employees. In 1976, a New Jersey court determined that an employer had a duty to shield its employees from the noxious effects of smoking. The case arose after Donna Shimp sued her employer, New Jersey Bell Telephone Company, for failing to protect her from cigarette smoke.

Shimp alleged that cigarette smoke at work caused her to suffer severe throat irritation, nasal irritation, eye irritation, headaches, nausea, and vomiting. The Superior Court of New

Jersey determined that the telephone company must enforce a no-smoking policy. It declared: "There can be no doubt that the by-products of burning tobacco are toxic and dangerous to the health of smokers and nonsmokers generally and this plaintiff in particular."[9]

The court cited evidence from the U.S. Surgeon General as well as experts in cardiovascular disease, allergy and immunology, and occupational safety in making its findings. "The employees' right to a safe working environment makes it clear that smoking must be forbidden in the work area," the judge wrote.[10]

> • Was the *Shimp* case properly decided? Should workers have the right to smoke at work? Does your employer or school allow students to smoke?

Other courts have determined that employees can sue to force their employers to prohibit or limit smoking in the workplace. In 2003, a federal appeals court reinstated a suit brought by a federal railroad worker who alleged that his severe asthma was exacerbated by his employer's refusal to enforce its no-smoking policy. A lower court had dismissed the employee's suit because the employee failed to present scientific evidence concerning the harmful effects of secondhand smoke. The appeals court reversed this decision, noting that the employer did not dispute that secondhand smoke is harmful. "While the duty to provide a reasonably safe workplace may not always be breached by the presence of second-hand smoke, we cannot accept the proposition that it can never be breached by an employer's failure to abate second-hand cigarette smoke in the workplace that aggravates a plaintiff's existing lung disease," the court wrote.[11]

Smoking bans should be imposed in other public places.

Many state and local clean indoor air laws, or antismoking regulations, have been upheld by many courts. Some states began passing antismoking legislation in the 1970s. Arizona passed such a law in 1973. It banned smoking in many public places, including elevators, libraries, theaters, and buses. In 1975, Minnesota passed its State Clean Indoor Air Act, which

FROM THE BENCH

Shimp v. *New Jersey Bell Telephone Company*, 145 N.J. Super. 516, 368 A.2d 408 (1976)

Employer's refusal to enact work place smoking ban denies nonsmoking employee who is severely allergic to gases produced by burning cigarettes her common-law right to safe working environment.

This case involves a matter of first impression in New Jersey: whether a non-smoking employee is denied a safe working environment and is entitled to injunctive relief when forced by proximity to smoking employees to involuntarily inhale "secondhand" cigarette smoke. The nonsmoking employee has severe allergic reaction to cigarette smoke. She alleges that her employer, the N.J. Bell Telephone Company, is causing her to work in an unsafe environment by refusing to ban smoking in the office where she is employed.

It is clearly the law of New Jersey that an employee has the right to work in a safe environment. An employer is under an affirmative duty to provide a work area that is free from unsafe conditions. This right to safe and healthful working conditions is protected not only by the duty imposed by common law upon employers but also by the Occupational Safety and Health Act, 29 U.S.C. § §651-78. OSHA in no way preempts the field of occupational safety. 29 U.S.C. § 653 (b) (4) recognizes concurrent state power to act either legislatively or judicially under common law with regard to occupational safety.

The nonsmoking employee has a common-law right to a safe working environment. The issue remains whether the work area here is unsafe due to a preventable hazard that the court may enjoin. There can be no doubt that the byproducts of burning tobacco are toxic and dangerous to the health of smokers and non-smokers generally, and to this employee in particular.

The national policy to warn the public of the dangerous nature of cigarette smoke, as expressed in the Public Health Cigarette Smoking Act, 15 U.S.C. § §1331 et seq., has made that fact generally acceptable. The court takes judicial notice of the toxic nature of cigarette smoke and its well-known association with emphysema, lung cancer, and heart disease.

prohibited smoking in many public places and workplaces. Today, most states have passed so-called clean indoor air laws to limit smoking in public places. These laws generally restrict, or

The HEW Report for 1975, The Health Consequences of Smoking, indicates that the more presence of cigarette smoke in the air pollutes it, changing carbon monoxide levels and effectively making involuntary smokers of all who breathe air. Prior to this report, it was generally accepted that smoking is a hazard voluntarily undertaken. The opinion that tobacco smoke should be eliminated from the work environment is shared by allergists, immunologists and specialists in the field of industrial medicine.

The evidence is clear and overwhelming. Cigarette smoke contaminates and pollutes the air creating a health hazard not merely to the smoker but to all those around the smoker who must rely upon the same air supply. The right of an individual to risk his or her own health does not include the right to jeopardize the health of those who must remain around him or her in order to properly perform the duties of their jobs. The portion of the population that is especially sensitive to cigarette smoke is so significant that it is reasonable to expect an employer to foresee health consequences and to impose upon the employer a duty to abate the hazard causing the discomfort.

The employees' right to a safe working environment makes it clear that smoking must be forbidden in the work area. The employee who desires to smoke on his or her own time, during coffee breaks and lunch hours, should have a reasonably accessible area to smoke. Such a rule imposes no hardship upon the telephone company.

The company already has in effect a rule that cigarettes are not to be smoked around telephone equipment. The rationale behind the rule is that the machines are extremely sensitive and can be damaged by the smoke. Human beings are also very sensitive and can be damaged by cigarette smoke. Unlike a piece of machinery, the damage to a human is all too often irreparable. If a circuit or wiring goes bad, the company can install a replacement part. It is not so simple in the case of a human lung, eye, or heart. The parts are hard to come by, if indeed they can be found at all. A company that has demonstrated such concern for its mechanical components should have at least as much concern for its human beings.

PUBLIC SMOKING BANS

Coastal states snuffing out cigarettes

Smoking bans in public places have appeared mostly in the Northeast and West Coast. Four states — California, Delaware, New York and Florida — ban smoking in all restaurants. Statewide bans begin in Connecticut in October and Maine in January [2004].

State-wide smoking bans and municipalities with smoke-free bar ordinances

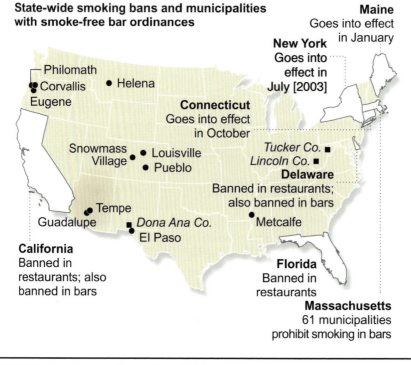

Maine
Goes into effect in January

New York
Goes into effect in July [2003]

Philomath
Corvallis
Eugene
Helena

Connecticut
Goes into effect in October

Snowmass Village
Louisville
Pueblo

Tucker Co.
Lincoln Co.

Delaware
Banned in restaurants; also banned in bars

Metcalfe

Tempe
Guadalupe
Dona Ana Co.
El Paso

California
Banned in restaurants; also banned in bars

Florida
Banned in restaurants

Massachusetts
61 municipalities prohibit smoking in bars

SOURCE: Americans for Nonsmokers' Rights   AP

In recent years, many states and local communities have enacted some form of ban on public smoking. This map created in July 2003 shows that the majority of smoking bans have been put into effect first in states on the nation's coasts, although states all over the country are following suit.

even ban entirely, smoking in many public places. They often allow smoking only in certain designated areas.

> • **Does your state have a clean indoor air law?**

In *City of Tucson* v. *Grezaffi*, an Arizona appeals court upheld a city law limiting smoking in restaurants.[12] The ordinance

(continued on page 38)

THE LETTER OF THE LAW

Florida Clean Indoor Air Act

2003 FL H.B. 63

Be It Enacted by the Legislature of the State of Florida:

Section 1. Section 386.201, Florida Statutes, is amended to read:

386.201 Popular name Short title .—This part may be cited by the popular name as the "Florida Clean Indoor Air Act."

Section 2. Section 386.202, Florida Statutes, is amended to read:

386.202 Legislative intent.—The purpose of this part is to protect people from the public health hazards of second-hand, comfort, and environment by creating areas in public places and at public meetings that are reasonably free from tobacco smoke and to implement the Florida health initiative in s. 20, Art. X of the State Constitution by providing a uniform statewide maximum code . It is the intent of the Legislature to not inhibit, or otherwise obstruct, medical or scientific research or smoking-cessation programs approved by the Department of Health. This part shall not be interpreted to require the designation of smoking areas. However, it is the intent of the Legislature to discourage the designation of any area within a government building as a smoking area....

Section 4. Section 386.204, Florida Statutes, is amended to read:

386.204 Prohibition.—A person may not smoke in an enclosed indoor workplace, except as otherwise provided in s. 386.2045 a public place or at a public meeting except in designated smoking areas. These prohibitions do not apply in cases in which an entire room or hall is used for a private function and seating arrangements are under the control of the sponsor of the function and not of the proprietor or person in charge of the room or hall.

Section 5. Section 386.2045, Florida Statutes, is created to read:

386.2045 Enclosed indoor workplaces; specific exceptions.—Notwithstanding s. 386.204, tobacco smoking may be permitted in each of the following places:

(1) PRIVATE RESIDENCE.—A private residence whenever it is not being used commercially to provide child care, adult care, or health care, or any combination thereof as defined in s. 386.203(1).

(2) RETAIL TOBACCO SHOP.—An enclosed indoor workplace dedicated to or predominantly for the retail sale of tobacco, tobacco products, and accessories for such products, as defined in s. 386.203(8).

(3) DESIGNATED SMOKING GUEST ROOM.—A designated smoking guest room at a public lodging establishment as defined in s. 386.203(4).

(4) STAND-ALONE BAR.—A business that meets the definition of a stand-alone bar as defined in s. 386.203(11) and that otherwise complies with all applicable provisions of the Beverage Law and part II of this chapter.

(5) SMOKING-CESSATION PROGRAM, MEDICAL OR SCIENTIFIC RESEARCH.—An enclosed indoor workplace, to the extent that tobacco smoking is an integral part of a smoking-cessation program approved by the department, or medical or scientific research conducted therein. Each room in which tobacco smoking is permitted must comply with the signage requirements in s. 386.206.

(6) CUSTOMS SMOKING ROOM.—A customs smoking room in an airport in-transit lounge under the authority and control of the Bureau of Customs and Border Protection of the United States Department of Homeland Security subject to the restrictions contained in s. 386.205.

Section 6. Section 386.205, Florida Statutes, is amended to read:

386.205 Customs Designation of smoking rooms areas .—

(1) A customs smoking room areas may be designated by the person in charge of an airport in-transit lounge under the authority and control of the Bureau of Customs and Border Protection of the United States Department of Homeland Security a public place. A customs smoking room may only be designated in an airport in-transit lounge under the

authority and control of the Bureau of Customs and Border Protection of the United States Department of Homeland Security....

(2) (a) A smoking area may not be designated in an elevator, school bus, public means of mass transportation subject only to state smoking regulation, restroom, hospital, doctor's or dentist's waiting room, jury deliberation room, county health department, day care center, school or other educational facility, or any common area.... However, a patient's room in a hospital, nursing home, or other health care facility may be designated as a smoking area if such designation is ordered by the attending physician and agreed to by all patients assigned to that room.

(b) Notwithstanding anything in this part to the contrary, no more than one-half of the rooms in any health care facility may be designated as smoking areas.

(3) In a workplace where there are smokers and nonsmokers, employers shall develop, implement, and post a policy regarding designation of smoking and nonsmoking areas. Such a policy shall take into consideration the proportion of smokers and nonsmokers. Employers who make reasonable efforts to develop, implement, and post such a policy shall be deemed in compliance. An entire area may be designated as a smoking area if all workers routinely assigned to work in that area at the same time agree....

Section 7. Section 386.206, Florida Statutes, is amended to read:

386.206 Posting of signs; requiring policies .—

(1) The person in charge of an enclosed indoor workplace that prior to adoption of s. 20, Art. X of the State Constitution was required to post signs under the requirements of this section must continue to a public place shall conspicuously post, or cause to be posted, in any area designated as a smoking area signs stating that smoking is not permitted in the enclosed indoor workplace such area . Each sign posted pursuant to this section must shall have letters of reasonable size which can be easily read. The color, design, and precise place of posting of such signs shall be left to the discretion of the person in charge of the premises. In order to increase public awareness, the person in charge of a public place may, at his or her discretion, also post "NO SMOKING EXCEPT IN DESIGNATED AREAS" signs as appropriate.

(2) The proprietor or other person in charge of an enclosed indoor workplace must develop and implement a policy regarding the smoking prohibitions established in this part. The policy may include, but is not limited to, procedures to be taken when the proprietor or other person in charge witnesses or is made aware of a violation of s. 386.204 in the enclosed indoor workplace and must include a policy which prohibits an employee from smoking in the enclosed indoor workplace. In order to increase public awareness, the person in charge of an enclosed indoor workplace may, at his or her discretion, post "NO SMOKING" signs as deemed appropriate.

(3) The person in charge of an airport terminal that includes a designated customs smoking room must conspicuously post, or cause to be posted, signs stating that no smoking is permitted except in the designated customs smoking room located in the customs area of the airport. Each sign posted pursuant to this section must have letters of reasonable size that can be easily read. The color, design, and precise locations at which such signs are posted shall be left to the discretion of the person in charge of the premises.

(4) The proprietor or other person in charge of an enclosed indoor workplace where a smoking cessation program, medical research, or scientific research is conducted or performed must conspicuously post, or cause to be posted, signs stating that smoking is permitted for such purposes in designated areas in the enclosed indoor workplace. Each sign posted pursuant to this section must have letters of reasonable size which can be easily read. The color, design, and precise locations at which such signs are posted shall be left to the discretion of the person in charge of the premises....

Section 9. Section 386.208, Florida Statutes, is amended to read:

386.208 Penalties.—Any person who violates s. 386.204 commits a non-criminal violation as defined provided for in s. 775.08(3), punishable by a fine of not more than $100 for the first violation and not more than $500 for each subsequent violation. Jurisdiction shall be with the appropriate county court.

Section 10. Section 386.209, Florida Statutes, is reenacted to read:

386.209 Regulation of smoking preempted to state.—This part expressly preempts regulation of smoking to the state and supersedes any municipal or county ordinance on the subject.

Section 11. Section 386.211, Florida Statutes, is amended to read:

386.211 Public announcements in mass transportation terminals.— Announcements about the Florida Clean Indoor Air Act shall be made regularly over public address systems in terminals of public transportation carriers located in metropolitan statistical areas with populations over 230,000 according to the latest census. These announcements shall be made at least every 30 minutes and shall be made in appropriate languages. Each announcement must shall include a statement to the effect that Florida is a clean indoor air state and that smoking is not allowed except as provided in this part only in designated areas .

Section 12. Section 386.212, Florida Statutes, is reenacted and amended to read:

386.212 Smoking prohibited near school property; penalty.—

(1) It is unlawful for any person under 18 years of age to smoke tobacco in, on, or within 1,000 feet of the real property comprising a public or private elementary, middle, or secondary school between the hours of 6 a.m. and midnight. This section does shall not apply to any person occupying a moving vehicle or within a private residence. . . .

Section 15. If any provision of this act or the application thereof to any person or circumstance is held invalid, the invalidity shall not affect other provisions or applications of the act which can be given effect without the invalid provision or application, and to this end the provisions of this act are declared severable.

Section 16. If any law amended by this act was also amended by a law enacted at the 2003 Regular Session of the Legislature, such laws shall be construed as if they had been enacted during the same session of the Legislature, and full effect shall be given to each if possible.

Section 17. This act shall take effect July 1, 2003.

(continued from page 33)

generally provided that "all restaurants shall be smokefree." The ordinance made it unlawful for restaurant operators or managers to allow smoking in restaurants except for in designated smoking areas, or to "allow smoke from a designated smoking area to diffuse or drift into a non-smoking area."

A group of restaurant owners challenged the constitutionality of the ordinance on several grounds. They argued, for instance, that the law infringed on the First Amendment right of freedom of association, violated the equal protection clause by singling out restaurants, and could be categorized as an unconstitutional "special" law. The appeals court determined that all of these constitutional challenges were meritless.

FROM THE BENCH

City of Tucson v. Grezaffi, 23 P.3d 675 (Ariz.App. 2001)

Restaurant owner was held responsible by magistrate for violation of city's restaurant smoking ordinance, and restaurant owner appealed.... The Court of Appeals, Pelander, J., held that: (1) review was limited to whether ordinance was constitutional on its face; (2) city had authority under city charter to promulgate ordinance banning smoking in restaurants; (3) ordinance was not preempted by state statutes....

City ordinance that promoted public welfare by prohibiting smoking in restaurants was a rational, legitimate means of safeguarding the general health, safety, and welfare of the community and did not violate restaurant owner's equal protection rights, though ordinance did not apply to other establishments, such as bars, bowling alleys or billiard halls....

In October 1999, Grezaffi was cited on a civil infraction for having violated Code § 11–19 (E) (2) which ... prohibits restaurant owners from allowing persons to smoke in restaurants except in a designated smoking area and from allowing smoke to diffuse or drift from a designated smoking area into a nonsmoking area. After an evidentiary hearing, a Tucson City Court magistrate found Grezaffi responsible, imposed a fine or community service, and ordered her to abate the violation....

> • **Should the owner of a bar be able to determine for his or her customers whether to allow smoking?**

The federal government has eliminated smoking on nearly all domestic flights since 1990. Federal law provides: "An individual may not smoke in an aircraft in scheduled passenger interstate air transportation or scheduled passenger intrastate air transportation."[13] This rule was not always the case. In fact, in 1971, a federal appeals court rejected a claim by consumer advocate Ralph Nader challenging smoking on aircraft flights. The court responded that the freedom to smoke had been "enjoyed by millions of passengers since the

(continued on page 42)

Contrary to Grezaffi's contention, we have no difficulty concluding that the ordinance is "rationally and reasonably related to furthering some legitimate governmental interest." . . . Significant scientific evidence suggests that smoking or exposure to second-hand smoke poses serious and substantial health risks. Grezaffi does not contest that proposition. Because the ordinance's goal of promoting the public welfare by alleviating smoke-related health concerns in restaurants is self-evident, "we need look no further." . . . The ordinance unquestionably is a reasonable, legitimate means of "safeguarding the general health, safety, and welfare of the community." . . .

[T]he ordinance bears a rational relationship to a legitimate, legislative purpose: preservation of the citizenry's health, comfort, safety, and welfare. Second, the ordinance applies "uniformly to all cases and to all members within the circumstances provided for by the law," that is, to all restaurants within the city. . . . Third, the ordinance is elastic because it permits restaurants to enter or exit its coverage depending on whether they have or no longer have certain specified characteristics. All restaurants in Tucson must comply with the ordinance's requirements. . . .

All of Grezaffi's constitutional challenges to the City's restaurant smoking ordinance are without merit. Code § 11–19 is facially valid. Accordingly, the superior court's order denying Grezaffi's appeal is affirmed.

THE LETTER OF THE LAW

From the Legislature: Utah Code Ann. Section 78-38-5, 78-38-1

78-38-5 Legislative intent.

(1) The Legislature finds:

   (a) the federal Environmental Protection Agency (EPA) has determined that environmental tobacco smoke is a Group A carcinogen, in the same category as other cancer-causing chemicals such as asbestos;

   (b) the EPA has determined that there is no acceptable level of exposure to Class A carcinogens; and

   (c) the EPA has determined that exposure to environmental tobacco smoke also causes an increase in respiratory diseases and disorders among exposed persons.

(2) The Legislature finds that environmental tobacco smoke generated in a rental or condominium unit may drift into other units, exposing the occupants of those units to tobacco smoke, and that standard construction practices are not effective in preventing this drift of tobacco smoke.

(3) The Legislature further finds that persons who desire to not be exposed to drifting environmental tobacco smoke should be able to determine in advance of entering into a rental, lease, or purchase agreement whether the subject unit may be exposed to environmental tobacco smoke.

1997

78-38-1 Nuisance defined—Right of action for—Judgment.

(1) A nuisance is anything which is injurious to health, indecent, offensive to the senses, or an obstruction to the free use of property, so as to interfere with the comfortable enjoyment of life or property. A nuisance may be the subject of an action.

(2) A nuisance may include the following:

   (a) drug houses and drug dealing ...

   (b) gambling ...

   (c) criminal activity committed in concert with two or more persons...

   (d) party houses...

   (e) prostitution ...

(3) A nuisance under this section includes tobacco smoke that drifts into any residential unit a person rents, leases, or owns, from another residential or commercial unit and this smoke:

   (a) drifts in more than once in each of two or more consecutive seven-day periods; and

   (b) creates any of the conditions under Subsection (1)....

(9) A cause of action for a nuisance under Subsection (3) may be brought against:

   (a the individual generating the tobacco smoke;

   (b) the renter or lessee who permits or fails to control the generation of tobacco smoke, in violation of the terms of his rental or lease agreement, on the premises he rents or leases; or

   (c) the landlord, but only if:

      (i) the terms of the renter's or lessee's contract provide the unit will not be subject to the nuisance of drifting tobacco smoke;

      (ii) the complaining renter or lessee has provided to the landlord a statement in writing indicating that tobacco smoke is creating a nuisance in the renter's or lessee's unit; and

      (iii) the landlord knowingly allows the continuation of a nuisance under Subsection (3) after receipt of written notice ... and in violation of the terms of the rental or lease agreement under Subsection (c)(i).

(continued from page 39)

advent of commercial aviation" and that "the freedom to smoke may have to give way to the freedom of others to be unannoyed by smoke but that is not a safety problem." [14]

The push to regulate smoking now extends even to the home. Many courts are looking at smoking as a factor in custody

FROM THE BENCH

Helling v. *McKinney*, 509 U.S. 25 (1993)

Respondent McKinney, a Nevada state prisoner, filed suit against petitioner prison officials, claiming that his involuntary exposure to environmental tobacco smoke (ETS) from his cellmate's and other inmates' cigarettes posed an unreasonable risk to his health, thus subjecting him to cruel and unusual punishment in violation of the Eighth Amendment. A federal magistrate granted petitioners' motion for a directed verdict, but the Court of Appeals reversed in part, holding that McKinney should have been permitted to prove that his ETS exposure was sufficient to constitute an unreasonable danger to his future health. It reaffirmed its decision after this Court remanded for further consideration in light of *Wilson* v. *Seiter, 501 U.S. 294*, in which the Court held that Eighth Amendment claims arising from confinement conditions not formally imposed as a sentence for a crime require proof of a subjective component, and that, where the claim alleges inhumane confinement conditions or failure to attend to a prisoner's medical needs, the standard for that state of mind is the "deliberate indifference" standard of *Estelle* v. *Gamble, 429 U.S. 97*. The Court of Appeals held that *Seiter*'s subjective component did not vitiate that court's determination that it would be cruel and unusual punishment to house a prisoner in an environment exposing him to ETS levels that pose an unreasonable risk of harming his health—the objective component of McKinney's claim.

Held:

1. It was not improper for the Court of Appeals to decide the question whether McKinney's claim could be based on possible future effects of ETS. From its examination of the record, the court was apparently of the view that the claimed entitlement to a smoke-free environment subsumed the claim that ETS exposure could endanger one's future, not just current, health.

2. By alleging that petitioners have, with deliberate indifference, exposed him to ETS levels that pose an unreasonable risk to his future health,

determinations between parents. One commentator writes: "When a child's environment subjects him or her to harm through the inhalation of dangerous substances, precautionary measures should not only be taken into account but regulated to ensure the child's best interests are met."[15]

McKinney has stated an Eighth Amendment claim on which relief could be granted. An injunction cannot be denied to inmates who plainly prove an unsafe, life-threatening condition on the ground that nothing yet has happened to them. . . . Thus, petitioners' central thesis that only deliberate indifference [509 U.S. 25, 26] to inmates' current serious health problems is actionable is rejected. Since the Court cannot at this juncture rule that McKinney cannot possibly prove an Eighth Amendment violation based on ETS exposure, it also would be premature to base a reversal on the Federal Government's argument that the harm from ETS exposure is speculative, with no risk sufficiently grave to implicate a serious medical need, and that the exposure is not contrary to current standards of decency. On remand, the District Court must give McKinney the opportunity to prove his allegations, which will require that he establish both the subjective and objective elements necessary to prove an Eighth Amendment violation. With respect to the objective factor, he may have difficulty showing that he is being exposed to unreasonably high ETS levels, since he has been moved to a new prison and no longer has a cellmate who smokes, and since a new state prison policy restricts smoking to certain areas and makes reasonable efforts to respect nonsmokers' wishes with regard to double bunking. He must also show that the risk of which he complains is not one that today's society chooses to tolerate. The subjective factor, deliberate indifference, should be determined in light of the prison authorities' current attitudes and conduct, which, as evidenced by the new smoking policy, may have changed considerably since the Court of Appeals' judgment. The inquiry into this factor also would be an appropriate vehicle to consider arguments regarding the realities of prison administration.

959 F.2d 853, affirmed and remanded.

- **Should parents lose custody if they smoke in front of their children?**

Law professor David Ezra argues in a 2001 law review article that "current law allows landlords, property managers, and homeowners associations to restrict or eliminate smoking, even in the friendly confines of one's own home."[16] He cites a Utah state law that allows condominium associations to declare tobacco smoking a nuisance.

Smoking bans should apply to prisons.

The movement to limit ETS exposure has even been extended to prisons. In 1993, the U.S. Supreme Court ruled in *Helling* v. *McKinney* that an inmate could sue prison officials for exposure to ETS.[17] William McKinney, a Nevada inmate, sued prison officials after they placed him in a cell with another inmate who smoked five packs of cigarettes a day. McKinney alleged that the prison officials subjected him to cruel and unusual punishment in violation of the Eighth Amendment by forcing him to live with a smoker. He contended that prison officials were showing deliberate indifference to his health by intentionally exposing him to high levels of ETS.

- **Should prison wardens have to keep inmates safe from high levels of smoke?**

Prison officials countered that McKinney could not sue them for any future harm the exposure to smoke might cause him because any such harm would be speculative. They said that McKinney could not recover damages unless he could show that he was currently suffering serious medical problems associated with exposure to tobacco smoke. The Court rejected that argument, writing: "It would be odd to deny an injunction to inmates who plainly proved an unsafe, life-threatening condition in their prison on the ground that nothing yet had happened to them."[18]

Some correctional institutes responded to this decision by banning smoking in their prisons. Some inmates sued the prison officials, contending that the smoking bans violated their constitutional rights. One federal court in Maryland ruled that state prison officials, in light of the Supreme Court's decision in *Helling*, could ban smoking. "It should be perfectly obvious to any rational person that the State of Maryland, in view of the well-known harmful effects of secondhand smoke, has a legitimate interest in protecting the health of nonsmokers forced to be its guests in correctional facilities," the court wrote. "In fact, the Supreme Court has held that state actors could face liability under section 1983 if they do not protect nonsmokers from smokers' secondhand smoke." [19]

A significant body of scientific evidence—from both the public and private sectors—establishes that exposure to environmental tobacco smoke presents serious health hazards for nonsmokers. This evidence also establishes that ETS exposure presents severe risks for children. Since the 1970s, society has increasingly recognized the rights of nonsmokers through a variety of measures. State and local legislators have passed a series of clean indoor air laws. Several courts have recognized that employers have a duty to protect nonsmoking employees from health hazards associated with smokers. The U.S. Supreme Court weighed in on the issue in a prisoner civil rights case, refusing to dismiss a lawsuit by a prisoner who alleged that he was facing potential health threats by being subjected to high levels of ETS exposure. In the last ten years, courts have determined that smoking is a pertinent factor in child custody decisions. There is now a movement to limit smoking in multi-unit residences. The writing is on the wall—smoking bans are legal and necessary.

Smoking Bans Infringe on Smokers' Individual Rights

Indeed, the [smoking] bans are symptoms of a far more grievous threat, a cancer that has been spreading for decades and has now metastasized throughout the body politic, spreading even to the tiniest organs of local government. This cancer is the only real hazard involved—the cancer of unlimited government power.
—Columnist Robert W. Tracinski[1]

In England in 2001, forty-one-year-old sales executive Mark Hodges was fired on the second day of his job because his company had instituted a no-smoking policy for employees. Although Hodges had been informed of the policy when he interviewed for the position, he said he had assumed that the policy was in effect only when he was at the office or in his company car. Hodges had not smoked in either of these places. He had smoked at home.

As Hodges explained, "I was sacked for smoking in my free

46

time. I am angry and astounded I could be treated like that."
In response to the incident, Ben Williams, a spokesperson for
Forest, a British smokers' rights group, said, "We know of cases
in the U.S. where employees have been breathalysed when they
got to work. This is a very extreme case but it does serve as an
example [of where] cases may go in the future."[2]

Many legal activities in society are dangerous, including
riding a motorcycle, skydiving, eating fatty foods, and even
working too hard. In a free society, individuals are given the
choice to engage in a variety of activities that may not be
the best decision. Some people believe that state restrictions
on smoking amount to a form of "legal paternalism" that
infringes on the fundamental right to liberty enshrined in the
Declaration of Independence.[3]

> • **Is smoking different from other dangerous activities? In a free society, should people have the right to choose whether to smoke?**

The rush to regulate tobacco has drawn comparisons to
the era of Prohibition, when the Eighteenth Amendment
amended the U.S. Constitution to ban the making and
selling of alcohol. "Ultimately some of the worst social
costs come not from drinking or smoking, but from the
enormous social, political, economic, and moral consequences
of going too far in limiting behavior," writes Mark Edward
Lender in his article "The New Prohibition."[4] Prohibition proved
to be an abject failure, as people continued to consume
alcohol. It seems to be the same way with cigarettes. People
will continue to smoke no matter what regulations are put
into place.

The EPA study on secondhand smoke is questionable.

Some studies have questioned whether environmental tobacco
smoke causes heart disease or lung cancer. One 1998 study

from the *Journal of the National Cancer Institute* concluded that there was not a statistically significant connection between exposure to secondhand smoke and lung cancer: "Our results indicate no association between childhood exposure to ETS and lung cancer risk. We did find weak evidence of a dose-response relationship between risk of lung cancer and exposure to spousal and workplace ETS. There was no detectable risk after cessation of exposure."[5]

"It seems unlikely that secondhand smoke presents any significant harm to otherwise healthy nonsmoking adults," says tobacco giant R.J. Reynolds. The company adds:

> An individual's risk for contracting a smoking-related disease is based on many factors in addition to smoking. . . . Considering all of the evidence, in our opinion, it seems unlikely that secondhand smoke presents any significant harm to otherwise healthy nonsmoking adults at the very low concentrations commonly encountered in homes, offices and other places where smoking is allowed.[6]

When the EPA issued its report classifying secondhand smoke as a carcinogen, responsible for causing three thousand deaths per year, several tobacco companies challenged the report in a federal lawsuit. The companies argued that the EPA failed to follow proper procedure and altered its methodology to reach a desired result. According to the tobacco companies, the EPA also wrongfully failed to include a tobacco industry representative on the advisory committee for the study.

In 1999, federal district court judge William Osteen agreed with the tobacco companies in *Flue-Cured Tobacco Cooperative Stabilization Corporation* v. *United States Environmental Protection Agency*.[7] He found there was substantial evidence that the EPA had "cherry-picked" among various studies and altered its own standards to reach a certain result. "Using its normal methodology and its selected studies, EPA did not demonstrate a statistically significant association between ETS and lung cancer," Judge Osteen wrote. "Instead, EPA changed its methodology to find a statistically significant association."[8]

• **Do you think the judge makes a good case against the EPA?**

Osteen concluded that the "EPA's conduct left substantial holes in the administrative record" and that "EPA produced limited evidence, then claimed the weight of the Agency's research evidence demonstrated ETS causes cancer."[9]

A federal appeals court reversed Judge Osteen's decision but did not dispute his findings. The appeals court determined that the tobacco companies could not challenge the EPA's report in federal court because the federal court did not have jurisdiction over an agency report that was not "final agency action" within the meaning of federal administrative law. However, even the federal appeals court seemed disturbed by the EPA's conduct, writing that "exclusion by the EPA of any meaningful tobacco industry representative from the advisory committee . . . is unexplained."[10]

The controversy over the EPA's handling of its report about secondhand smoke caused one commentator to write: "Despite the rhetoric of the anti-tobacco industry, science does not back up the ETS scare campaign."[11]

Many smoking bans were passed without proper authority.

Many cities and counties have passed smoking bans even when they did not possess the authority to do so. In 2003, a legal dispute brewed in the state of New York over a law that bans smoking in many public places, including bars and taverns. A group of bar and tavern associations, led by the Empire State Restaurant and Tavern Association, Inc., sued the state, contending that the law was unconstitutional.

In *Empire State Restaurant and Tavern Association* v. *New York State*, the plaintiffs alleged that the smoking ban violates due process, is preempted by federal law, and violates the supremacy clause of the U.S. Constitution. The plaintiffs contended that the New York State law conflicts with the federal regulations of the Occupational Safety and Health Administrations (OSHA) on worker exposure to tobacco smoke. In their complaint, they argue that the New York law's "broad ban on smoking in workplaces directly, substantially and specifically regulates occupational safety and health."[12]

Empire State argues that the federal law under OSHA preempts or trumps state law. Because the New York law regulates an area under federal control, the plaintiffs argue that it violates the supremacy clause of the Constitution, which provides that the federal laws of the United States "shall be the supreme Law of the Land." A federal district court judge refused to enjoin or stop enforcement of the law in October 2003, but the lawsuit continues.

> • **Do you think the Empire State group should succeed in its lawsuit?**

The Ohio supreme court recently ruled that a county board of health exceeded its authority when it passed a smoking ban. Such authority, reasoned the court, resided with the state legislature—not an administrative agency like the local health board. The court stated: "There is no express grant of power [in the state law] or elsewhere, allowing local boards of health unfettered authority to promulgate any health regulation deemed necessary."[13]

The phenomenon caused South Carolina State Senator John Graham Altman III to introduce a bill in June 2003 that would prohibit cities from passing smoking bans in restaurants and bars. The bill would provide that cities that ignored this provision would risk losing state funding. "This is an issue of government becoming more and more socialistic and telling the owners and operators of private property what they can and can't do," Altman told a Charleston newspaper.[14]

State smoking bans are not insulated from legal attacks either. The Empire Restaurant and Tavern Association has challenged the constitutionality of New York's state indoor smoking ban. The enforcement of the law has had a devastating financial impact on many taverns and bars. Another effect of the state law will be to force more smoking onto public streets, increasing the exposure to smoke for people walking the streets.

Some local officials have even sought to extend their local smoking bans to purely private establishments. In a Massachusetts case, city officials sought to enforce their smoking ban on a fraternal lodge. A state appeals court rejected the extension of the smoking ban on the lodge, a private establishment to which the general public did not have access.[15]

In October 2003, the West Virginia state supreme court heard arguments in a case that challenged a county smoking ban. The court will decide whether the state legislature gave county health boards the authority to regulate secondhand smoke. The county argues that the legislature gave the county health boards the power to regulate clean air and water, which includes the ability to regulate secondhand smoke. Lawyers for those challenging the ban contend that the county health boards do not have the power to regulate tobacco.[16] Also in October 2003, the Montana supreme court agreed to review a case challenging the validity of smoking bans in that state. These court decisions could eventually lead to a challenge before the U.S. Supreme Court.

Workers who smoke face discrimination.

The majority of states have passed laws prohibiting employers from firing workers who smoke off-duty or on breaks in specifically designated smoking areas. Such laws protect workers who follow the employer's guidelines about when and where they can smoke while on-duty. It also ensures that employers do not invade the private lives of their employees by regulating off-duty behavior.

> • **Does your state have a smokers' rights law? Do you believe there is discrimination against smokers in society?**

The Indiana Court of Appeals ruled that an employee was entitled to unemployment compensation when his employer fired him for violating a company rule prohibiting drinking and smoking while off-duty. The court wrote that "in order for an employer rule which regulates an employee's off-duty activity to be considered reasonable, the activity sought to be

THE LETTER OF THE LAW

From the Legislatures:

Tennessee: T.C.A. 50-1-304(e)

No employee shall be discharged or terminated solely for participating or engaging in the use of an agricultural product not regulated by the alcoholic beverage commission that is not otherwise proscribed by law, if such employee participates or engages in such use in a manner which complies with all applicable employer policies regarding such use during times at which such employee is working.

South Dakota 60-4-11 Discrimination against employee's off-duty use of tobacco

It is a discriminatory or unfair employment practice for an employer to terminate the employment of an employee due to that employee's engaging in any use of tobacco products off the premises of the employer during nonworking hours unless such a restriction:

(1) Relates to a bona fide occupational requirement and is reasonably and rationally related to the employment activities and responsibilities of a particular employee or a particular group of employees, rather than to all employees of the employer; or

(2) Is necessary to avoid a conflict of interest with any responsibilities to the employer or the appearance of such a conflict of interest.

regulated must bear some reasonable relationship to the employer's business interest." [17]

———•———————•———————•———

It has been established that smoking is bad for smokers. Even so, we live in a free society, and if we continue to allow the government unlicensed and unchecked authority to regulate private choices, we will no longer live in an age of individual responsibility. Many activities in life are dangerous or unhealthy, including various types of food and recreational activities.

The case against secondhand smoke, however, has been scientifically questionable. Some studies have found little, if any, statistical association between secondhand smoke and lung cancer. A federal judge ruled that the Environmental Protection Agency's 1993 report classifying secondhand smoke as a carcinogen was deeply flawed.

The push for smoking bans infringes on individual freedom of choice. Extending smoking bans to bars and outdoor establishments shows that society has now crossed the line toward discrimination against smokers. Many states have had to pass antismoking discrimination laws to protect smokers from outright discrimination in the workforce.

Suits Against Big Tobacco Are Legitimate Cases Against Wealthy Defendants Selling Harmful Products

In 1999, fifty-two year-old Patricia Henley was awarded a $51.5-million verdict by a California jury after suing Philip Morris for deliberately misrepresenting the dangers of smoking. Prior to being diagnosed with terminal lung cancer, Henley had smoked three packs of cigarettes a day since she began to smoke as a teenager. In response to the verdict, Henley said, "I feel wonderful. I went into this case figuring we'd never beat big business." She said that she intended to donate her damages money to help educate children about the risks of smoking.[1]

Lawsuits like Patricia Henley's have become more and more common over the past several years, and plaintiffs have often received enormous sums in their victories over the tobacco companies. After all, tobacco industry executives oversee a billion-dollar industry that causes horrible health hazards for its consumers. Tobacco producers have engaged in a pattern of deceitful behavior, concealing the level of harmfulness and addictiveness of their product. They have aggressively marketed an unreasonably dangerous product to the public.

The basics of tort law allow antitobacco suits.

In the American legal system, injured persons can sue those people who harm them in a civil action, known as a tort. For instance, if person A punches person B in the face, causing damage, B can sue A for the tort of battery (which may also be a crime). The person suing is called the plaintiff and the person being sued is called the defendant. In a tort suit, the defendant is sometimes referred to as the tortfeasor. There are three main categories of torts: (1) intentional torts; (2) torts of negligence; and (3) strict liability torts.

Intentional torts are those in which the defendant intended to bring about a certain result. Battery—when the defendant deliberately strikes the plaintiff with the goal of causing injury—is an example of an intentional tort.

Negligence refers to engaging in socially unreasonable conduct. A defendant does not have to intend for harm to occur to a victim in order to be negligent. For instance, if person A runs his or her car into person B's car, person A may be negligent and legally responsible even though he or she did not *intend* to hit the other car. Negligence cases require a plaintiff to prove duty, breach of duty, causation, and damage. Often, the most challenging aspects of tort cases are proving breach of duty and causation. To show breach of duty, a plaintiff must demonstrate that the defendant acted unreasonably or failed to adhere to a particular standard of care. Causation requires the plaintiff to show that the defendant's conduct was the actual and legal cause of the plaintiff's injuries. Tobacco companies will often argue that tobacco products were not the legal cause of the plaintiff's harm. They may claim that the plaintiff's own conduct in purchasing the cigarettes, the plaintiff's own unhealthy eating habits, or the plaintiff's stressful work and home-life situations were the true cause of the plaintiff's health condition.

Finally, strict liability torts are those in which liability can be imposed without a showing of intent or negligence. Strict liability is sometimes used in products liability cases, where a defendant introduces unreasonably dangerous products into the marketplace.

Regardless of the type of tort lawsuit brought to court, the most common remedy the plaintiff seeks is monetary damages. There are two main types of damages: compensatory damages and punitive damages. Compensatory damages are designed to pay back the plaintiff for the harm that he or she suffered. Punitive damages, on the other hand, seek to punish the wrongdoer.

One of the most challenging and fascinating aspects of tort law is its application to the tobacco companies. Individuals and states have sued tobacco companies under a variety of tort theories. For example, products liability suits have been filed, claiming that cigarettes are an unreasonably dangerous product. Other cases have argued that the tobacco companies were negligent in how they represented their product. Many lawsuits fault the tobacco companies for failing to warn consumers about known dangers. Litigation against tobacco companies involves many claims. A few of the most common include fraudulent misrepresentation, negligence, failure to warn, conspiracy to conceal health information, and breach of express warranty.

> • **Should cigarettes be considered an unreasonably dangerous product? Should products liability laws apply to cigarettes?**

Early plaintiffs failed to defeat the tobacco industry.

Beginning in the 1950s, smokers or their close relatives began suing the tobacco companies, claiming that the companies should be liable for the harm that had befallen smokers. Experts have divided the litigation against the tobacco industry into three eras: (1) 1954–1973; (2) 1983–1992; and (3) 1994–present. Plaintiffs in the first wave of litigation often lost their cases because their attorneys could not conclusively prove the causation between smoking and disease.

Even in the second wave of litigation, the tobacco industry successfully argued that the smokers themselves were also at fault, or contributorily negligent. Only two dozen suits were filed against the tobacco industry in the 1970s and only one reached a jury, which ruled in favor of the tobacco companies. Under the doctrine of contributory negligence, a plaintiff could not recover damages from a defendant if the plaintiff was also at fault, or contributorily negligent.

> • **Why did the tobacco industry win in almost every early case?**

Gradually, most states moved from the doctrine of contributory negligence to a system called comparative negligence. Under a system of comparative negligence, juries apportion fault among all parties. For example, a jury might find that a tobacco company was 50 percent at fault for injuries to a smoker, but that the smoker was also 50 percent at fault. The industry also relied on the related assumption of risk doctrine. This concept holds that plaintiffs cannot sue for damages when they have assumed the risk of harmful activity.

F or 40 years, from 1954 to 1994, tobacco litigation provided the perfect example of David and Goliath litigation. Plaintiff after plaintiff was crushed by the tobacco defendants. Hundreds of claims were filed during those decades. The vast majority of the cases were dismissed before trial.

—Howard Erichson, Professor of Law, Seton Hall University

However, new medical studies provided nearly irrefutable proof that smoking caused cancer. Also, more documents from the tobacco companies established that the companies knew of the addictiveness of nicotine. The tobacco industry knew of the addictiveness of nicotine and concealed its knowledge of this, while making its products more addictive. This new information led to a third wave of litigation, with more promising results for plaintiffs. Law professor Richard L. Cupp, Jr., wrote that the new information about tobacco industry misconduct turned the tide for plaintiffs and will likely lead to more judgments for them.[2]

The *Cipollone* case sets a new standard.

In 1983, Rose Cipollone and her husband sued several tobacco companies, seeking to have them pay for damages she suffered as a smoker since 1942. She sued for fraudulent misrepresentation, conspiracy to deprive the public of needed health information about cigarettes, failure to warn the public about all health hazards, and breach of express warranty in their advertisements. Her express warranty claim was that the tobacco companies had "expressly warranted that smoking the cigarettes which they manufactured and sold did not present any significant health consequences."[3]

The tobacco company argued that the federal warning label required by federal law preempted any state law action for damages. The mandated label read: "WARNING: THE SURGEON GENERAL HAS DETERMINED THAT CIGARETTE SMOKING IS DANGEROUS TO YOUR HEALTH." The companies argued that this warning protected them from any lawsuits for conduct that took place after the warning.

> • **Should a smoker be able to sue tobacco companies if the companies place warning labels on their products?**

The companies argued that the federal warning statutes— the 1965 Federal Cigarette Labeling and Advertising Act and the

1969 Public Health Cigarette Smoking Act—preempted any state common law tort actions. A federal trial court rejected this preemption defense, but a federal appeals court accepted it. The court of appeals reasoned that federal law "preempts those state law damage actions relating to smoking and health that challenge either the adequacy of the warning on cigarette packages or the propriety of a party's actions with respect to the advertising and promotion of cigarettes."

The case went to back to the district court for trial and the district court, following the court of appeals' reasoning, dismissed the failure-to-warn, express-warranty, fraudulent-misrepresentation, and conspiracy-to-defraud claims. These allegations were barred to the extent that they relied on the tobacco companies' advertising activities after 1965. The plaintiffs were allowed to proceed with some of their claims based on the tobacco companies' conduct before 1965, however. The trial lasted for four months. The jury awarded $400,000 to Rose Cipollone's husband (by then, Rose herself had died of lung cancer) but found Rose 80 percent responsible for her own injuries. Even so, the jury did award her estate damages for the loss of warranty claim.

The court of appeals affirmed the lower court's preemption rulings but remanded for a new trial. The case was then appealed to the U.S. Supreme Court, which agreed to hear the case to resolve the preemption question.

The question before the Court concerned the effect of Section 5(b) of the 1969 Public Health Cigarette Smoking Act. That provision stated:

> No requirement or prohibition based on smoking and health
> shall be imposed under State law with respect to the advertis-
> ing or promotion of any cigarettes the packages of which are
> labeled in conformity with the provisions of this Act.

• **Should this provision preempt state tort law claims?**

(continued on page 65)

Cipollone v. Liggett Group, Inc., 505 U.S. 504 (1992)

Section 4 of the Federal Cigarette Labeling and Advertising Act (1965 Act) required a conspicuous label warning of smoking's health hazards to be placed on every package of cigarettes sold in this country, while 5 of that Act, captioned "Preemption," provided:"(a) No statement relating to smoking and health, other than the [4] statement ... , shall be required on any cigarette package," and (b) No [such] statement ... shall be required in the advertising of any cigarettes the packages of which are labeled in conformity with 4. Section 5(b) was amended by the Public Health Cigarette Smoking Act of 1969 (1969 Act) to specify: No requirement or prohibition based on smoking and health shall be imposed under State law with respect to the advertising or promotion of any cigarettes the packages of which are [lawfully] labeled." Petitioner's complaint in his action for damages invoked the District Court's diversity jurisdiction and alleged ... that respondent cigarette manufacturers were responsible for the 1984 death of his mother, a smoker since 1942, because they breached express warranties contained in their advertising, failed to warn consumers about smoking's hazards, fraudulently misrepresented those hazards to consumers, and conspired to deprive the public of medical and scientific information about smoking, all in derogation of duties created by New Jersey law. The District Court ultimately ruled, among other things, that these claims were preempted by the 1965 and 1969 Acts to the extent that the claims relied on respondents' advertising, promotional, and public relations activities after the effective date of the 1965 Act. The Court of Appeals affirmed on this point.

JUSTICE STEVENS delivered the opinion of the Court ...

"WARNING: THE SURGEON GENERAL HAS DETERMINED THAT CIGARETTE SMOKING IS DANGEROUS TO YOUR HEALTH." A federal statute enacted in 1969 requires that warning (or a variation thereof) to appear in a conspicuous place on every package of cigarettes sold in the United States. The questions presented to us by this case are whether that statute, or its 1965 predecessor which required a less alarming label, preempted petitioner's common-law claims against respondent cigarette manufacturers.

Petitioner is the son of Rose Cipollone, who began smoking in 1942 and who died of lung cancer in 1984. He claims that respondents are responsible for

Rose Cipollone's death because they breached express warranties contained in their advertising, because they failed to warn consumers about the hazards of smoking, because they fraudulently misrepresented those hazards to consumers, and because they conspired to deprive the public of medical and scientific information about smoking. The Court of Appeals held that petitioner's state-law claims were preempted by federal statutes, 893 F.2d 541 (CA3 1990), and other courts have agreed with that analysis. The highest court of the State New Jersey, however, has held that the federal statutes [505 U.S. 504, 509]   did not preempt similar common-law claims. Because of the manifest importance of the issue, we granted certiorari to resolve the conflict, *500 U.S. 499, 935* (1991). We now reverse in part and affirm in part.

On August 1, 1983, Rose Cipollone and her husband filed a complaint invoking the diversity jurisdiction of the Federal District Court. Their complaint alleged that Rose Cipollone developed lung cancer because she smoked cigarettes manufactured and sold by the three respondents. After her death in 1984, her husband filed an amended complaint. After trial, he also died; their son, executor of both estates, now maintains this action.

Petitioner's third amended complaint alleges several different bases of recovery, relying on theories of strict liability, negligence, express warranty, and intentional tort. These claims, all based on New Jersey law, divide into five categories. The "design defect claims" allege that respondents' cigarettes were defective because respondents failed to use a safer alternative design for their products and because the social value of their product was outweighed by the dangers it created (Count 2, App. 83 – 84). The "failure to warn claims" allege both that the product was "defective as a result of [respondents'] failure to provide adequate warnings of the health consequences of cigarette smoking" (Count 3, App. 85) and that respondents "were negligent in the manner [that] they tested, researched, sold, promoted and advertised" their cigarettes (Count 4, App. 86). The "express warranty claims" allege that respondents had "expressly [505 U.S. 504, 510] warranted that smoking the cigarettes which they manufactured and sold did not present any significant health consequences" (Count 7, App. 88). The "fraudulent misrepresentation claims" allege that respondents had willfully, "through their advertising, attempted to neutralize the [federally mandated] warnin[g]" labels (Count 6, App. 87–88), and that they had possessed, but had "ignored and failed to act upon," medical and scientific data indicating that "cigarettes were hazardous to the health of consumers" (Count 8, App. 89). Finally, the "conspiracy to defraud claims" allege that respondents conspired to deprive the public of such medical and scientific data (Ibid.). . . .

Although physicians had suspected a link between smoking and illness for centuries, the first medical studies of that connection did not appear until the 1920's. See U.S. Dept. of Health and Human Services, Report of the Surgeon General, Reducing the Health Consequences of Smoking: 25 Years of Progress 5 (1989). The ensuing decades saw a wide range of epidemiologic and laboratory studies on the health hazards of smoking. Thus, by the time the Surgeon General convened an advisory committee to examine the issue in 1962, there were more than 7,000 publications examining the relationship between smoking and health. . . .

In 1964, the advisory committee issued its report, which stated as its central conclusion: "Cigarette smoking is a health hazard of sufficient importance in the United States to warrant appropriate remedial action." . . . Relying in part on that report, the Federal Trade Commission (FTC), which had long regulated unfair and deceptive advertising practices in the cigarette industry, promulgated a new trade regulation rule. That rule, which was to take effect January 1, 1965, established that it would be a violation of the Federal Trade Commission Act "to fail to disclose, clearly and prominently, in all advertising and on every pack, box, carton, or container [of cigarettes] that cigarette smoking is dangerous to health and may cause death from cancer and other diseases." [T]he Act mandated warnings on cigarette packages (5(a)), but barred the requirement of such warnings in cigarette advertising (5(b)).

Section 2 of the Act declares the statute's two purposes: (1) adequately informing the public that cigarette smoking may be hazardous to health, and (2) protecting the national economy from the burden imposed by diverse, nonuniform, and confusing cigarette labeling and advertising regulations. In furtherance of the first purpose, 4 of the Act made it unlawful to sell or distribute any cigarettes in the United States unless the package bore a conspicuous label stating: "CAUTION: CIGARETTE SMOKING MAY BE HAZARDOUS TO YOUR HEALTH." In furtherance of the second purpose, 5, captioned "Preemption," provided in part:

"(a) No statement relating to smoking and health, other than the statement required by section 4 of this Act, shall be required on any cigarette package.

"(b) No statement relating to smoking and health shall be required in the advertising of any cigarettes the packages of which are labeled in conformity with the provisions of this Act." . . .

Although the Act took effect January 1, 1966, 10 of the Act provided that its provisions affecting the regulation of advertising would terminate on July 1, 1969....

It was in this context that Congress enacted the Public Health Cigarette Smoking Act of 1969 (1969 Act or Act), which amended the 1965 Act in several ways. First, the 1969 Act strengthened the warning label, in part by requiring a statement that cigarette smoking "is dangerous," rather than that it "may be hazardous." Second, the 1969 Act banned cigarette advertising in "any medium of electronic communication subject to [FCC] jurisdiction." Third, and related, the 1969 Act modified the preemption provision by replacing the original 5(b) with a provision that reads:

(b) No requirement or prohibition based on smoking and health shall be imposed under State law with respect to the advertising or promotion of any cigarettes the packages of which are labeled in conformity with the provisions of this Act....

In our opinion, the preemptive scope of the 1965 Act and the 1969 Act is governed entirely by the express language in 5 of each Act. When Congress has considered the issue of preemption and has included in the enacted legislation a provision explicitly addressing that issue, and when that provision provides a "reliable indicium of congressional intent with respect to state authority," *Malone* v. *White Motor Corp., 435 U.S., at 505* , "there is no need to infer congressional intent to preempt state laws from the substantive provisions" of the legislation....

For these reasons, we conclude that 5 of the 1965 Act only preempted state and federal rulemaking bodies from [505 U.S. 504, 520] mandating particular cautionary statements, and did not preempt state-law damages actions....

We consider each category of damages actions in turn. In doing so, we express no opinion on whether these actions are viable claims as a matter of state law; we assume ... that they are.

Failure to Warn

To establish liability for a failure to warn, petitioner must show that "a warning is necessary to make a product ... reasonably safe, suitable and fit for its intended use," that respondents failed to provide such a warning, and that that failure was a proximate cause of petitioner's injury. Tr. 12738. In this case, petitioner offered two closely related theories concerning the failure to warn: first, that respondents "were negligent in the manner [that] they tested, researched, sold, promoted, and advertised" their cigarettes; and second, that respondents failed to provide "adequate warnings of the health consequences of cigarette smoking." App. 85 – 86.

Petitioner's claims are preempted to the extent that they rely on a state-law "requirement or prohibition . . . with respect to . . . advertising or promotion." Thus, insofar as claims under either failure-to-warn theory require a showing that respondents' post-1969 advertising or promotions should have included additional, or more clearly stated, warnings, those claims are preempted. The Act does not, however, preempt petitioner's claims that rely solely on respondents' [505 U.S. 504, 525] testing or research practices or other actions unrelated to advertising or promotion....

Fraudulent Misrepresentation

Petitioner alleges two theories of fraudulent misrepresentation. First, petitioner alleges that respondents, through their advertising, neutralized the effect of federally mandated warning labels. Such a claim is predicated on a state-law prohibition against statements in advertising and promotional materials that tend to minimize the health hazards associated with smoking. Such a prohibition, however, is merely the converse of a state-law requirement that warnings be included in advertising and promotional materials. Section 5(b) of the 1969 Act preempts both requirements and prohibitions; it therefore supersedes petitioner's first fraudulent misrepresentation theory.

Regulators have long recognized the relationship between prohibitions on advertising that downplays the dangers of smoking and requirements for warnings in advertisements. For example, the FTC, in promulgating its initial trade regulation rule in 1964, criticized advertising that "associated cigarette smoking with such positive attributes as contentment, glamour, romance, youth, happiness . . . at the same time suggesting that smoking is an activity at least consistent with physical health and well-being." The Commission concluded:

> To avoid giving a false impression that smoking [is] innocuous, the cigarette manufacturer who represents the alleged pleasures or satisfactions of cigarette smoking in his advertising must also disclose the serious risks to life that smoking involves. 29 Fed. Reg. 8356 (1964)....

Conspiracy to Misrepresent or Conceal Material Facts

Petitioner's final claim alleges a conspiracy among respondents to misrepresent or conceal material facts concerning the health hazards of smoking. The predicate duty underlying this claim is a duty not to conspire to commit fraud....

To summarize our holding: the 1965 Act did not preempt state-law damages actions; the 1969 Act preempts petitioner's claims based on a failure to warn and the neutralization [505 U.S. 504, 531] federally mandated warnings to the extent that those claims rely on omissions or inclusions in respondents' advertising or promotions; the 1969 Act does not preempt petitioner's claims based on express warranty, intentional fraud and misrepresentation, or conspiracy.

The judgment of the Court of Appeals is accordingly reversed in part and affirmed in part, and the case is remanded for further proceedings consistent with this opinion.

It is so ordered.

(continued from page 59)

The Court determined that this provision preempted some of Cipollone's claims. The Court determined that her failure to warn claim was preempted to the extent that the claim stated that the companies should have provided additional or more clearly worded warnings about the health hazards of cigarettes. However, the Court reasoned that the act did not preempt claims related solely to the companies' "testing or research practices or other actions unrelated to advertising or promotion."[4]

The Court determined that Cipollone's breach of warranty claims were not preempted by federal law. The Court reasoned that federal law only preempted claims "imposed under State law." A warrant is not imposed under state law but by the specific warrantor, in this case, the tobacco company. As the Court explained, "In short, a common-law remedy for a contractual commitment voluntarily undertaken should not be regarded as a 'requirement . . . imposed under State law' within the meaning" of federal law.[5]

The Court also determined that some of Cipollone's other claims, including her conspiracy to misrepresent or conceal material facts claim, were not preempted. "Congress offered no sign that it wished to insulate cigarette manufacturers from long-standing rules governing fraud," the Court wrote.

FROM THE BENCH

Castano v. American Tobacco Co. 84 F. 3d 734 (5th Cir. 1996)

JERRY E. SMITH, Circuit Judge:

In what may be the largest class action ever attempted in federal court, the district court in this case embarked "on a road certainly less traveled, if ever taken at all," *Castano* v. *American Tobacco Co.*, 160 F.R.D. 544, 560 (E.D. La. 1995) (citing Edward C. Latham, *The Poetry of Robert Frost, "The Road Not Taken"* 105 (1969)), and entered a class certification order. The court defined the class as:

(a) All nicotine-dependent persons in the United States who have purchased and smoked cigarettes manufactured by the defendants;

(b) the estates, representatives, and administrators of these nicotine-dependent cigarette smokers; and

(c) the spouses, children, relatives and "significant others" of these nicotine-dependent cigarette smokers as their heirs or survivors....

This matter comes before us on interlocutory appeal, under 28 U.S.C. 1292(b), of the class certification order. Concluding that the district court abused its discretion in certifying the class, we reverse.

I.

A. The Class Complaint

The plaintiffs filed this class complaint against the defendant tobacco companies and the Tobacco Institute, Inc., seeking compensation solely for the injury of nicotine addiction.... The class compliant alleges nine causes of action: fraud and deceit, negligent misrepresentation, intentional infliction of emotional distress, negligence and negligent infliction of emotional distress, violation of state consumer protection statutes, breach of express warranty, breach of implied warranty, strict product liability, and redhibition pursuant to the Louisiana Civil Code.

Private suits have continued against Big Tobacco.

In 1994, a group of plaintiffs' attorneys joined together to pursue a nationwide class-action lawsuit against the tobacco industry. The group, called the Castano group, spurred other sets of attorneys and advocates to join forces to face the mighty

The plaintiffs seek compensatory and punitive damages and attorneys' fees....

The plaintiffs initially defined the class as "all nicotine dependent persons in the United States," including current, former and deceased smokers since 1943. Plaintiffs conceded that addiction would have to be proven by each class member; the defendants argued that proving class membership will require individual mini-trials to determine whether addiction actually exists....

II.

A district court must conduct a rigorous analysis of the rule 23 prerequisites before certifying a class.... The party seeking certification bears the burden of proof....

The district court erred in its analysis in two distinct ways. First, it failed to consider how variations in state law affect predominance and superiority. Second, its predominance inquiry did not include consideration of how a trial on the merits would be conducted.

Each of these defects mandates reversal....

In summary, whether the specter of millions of cases outweighs any manage-ability problems in this class is uncertain when the scope of any manageability problems is unknown. Absent considered judgment on the manageability of the class, a comparison to millions of individual trials is meaningless....

IV.

The district court abused its discretion by ignoring variations in state law and how a trial on the alleged causes of action would be tried. Those errors cannot be corrected on remand because of the novelty of the plaintiffs' claims. Accordingly, class treatment is not superior to individual adjudication.

We have once before stated that "traditional ways of proceeding reflect far more than habit. They reflect the very culture of the jury trial...." The collective wisdom of individual juries is necessary before this court commits the fate of an entire industry or, indeed, the fate of a class of millions, to a single jury. For the forgoing reasons, we REVERSE and REMAND with instructions that the district court dismiss the class complaint.

tobacco industry. On March 29, 1994, in *Castano* v. *American Tobacco Co.*, more than 60 law firms sued the tobacco industry in a class-action lawsuit for the "injury of nicotine addiction."[6]

A federal appeals court decertified the multistate class-action suit, pointing out that differences in state law and individual smokers made the case improper for a class-action suit: "The collective wisdom of individual juries is necessary before this court commits the fate of an entire industry or indeed, the fate of a class of millions, to a single jury."[7]

Since the late 1990s, several juries have tagged large tobacco companies with astronomical damage awards, including punitive damage awards, designed to punish the tobacco industry. The wealth of the defendant is a germane factor in a calculus of punitive damages.

Plaintiffs' chances seemed to grow in tobacco cases once it was revealed, sometimes through whistleblowers (individuals who expose company wrongdoing), that the tobacco company actively concealed the danger and addictiveness of their products. One federal district court explained: "it is not for making a dangerous product that defendant should be punished. It is for concealing how dangerous the product is that R.J. Reynolds merits punishment."[8]

> • **Does your state have a law protecting whistleblowers? Should tobacco companies pay punitive damages for concealing how dangerous cigarettes are? Do tobacco companies have a duty to disclose such information?**

In some cases, the tobacco industry has settled cases rather than risk a "runaway jury," or a jury that might impose astronomical punitive damage awards. For example, in 1997, tobacco manufacturers agreed to pay $349 million to settle a class-action lawsuit filed in Florida on behalf of sixty thousand flight attendants who allegedly suffered injuries from secondhand smoke on airplanes.

In 2002, the tobacco industry suffered some dramatic setbacks, including several huge punitive damages awards. These awards included one in *Bullock* v. *Philip Morris* for an astonishing $28 billion in punitive damages. A judge later reduced the award to $28 million. Another case resulted in a $150 million award and a third verdict was for $37.5 million.[9]

• **Do you think the jury in the *Bullock* case was a "runaway jury"?**

(continued on page 72)

FROM THE BENCH

Burton v. *R.J. Reynolds*, 205 F.Supp. 1253 (D. Kan. 2002)

Plaintiff filed this personal injury products liability action against defendant R.J. Reynolds Tobacco Company ("Reynolds") claiming that defendant's cigarettes caused his peripheral vascular disease ("PVD") and addiction. Plaintiff asserted that Reynolds manufactured a defective product, failed to warn him that smoking causes addiction and PVD, negligently failed to test or research its product, fraudulently concealed the fact that smoking cigarettes causes addiction and PVD, and conspired with other members of the tobacco industry to fraudulently conceal the health effects of smoking....

Having considered all of the evidence introduced in the trial of this case and the additional evidence which was admitted at the hearing on punitive damages, as well as the papers filed by the parties and the arguments of counsel, the court is now prepared to issue its ruling concerning the amount to be awarded as punitive damages in this case. For the reasons set forth below, the court directs the Clerk of the Court to modify and amend the judgment previously entered in this case to award plaintiff punitive damages in the amount of $15,000,000....

In this case, the jury found that the defendant R.J. Reynolds should be punished for its fraudulent concealment of information concerning the addictive nature of its product and its propensity to cause PVD. That conduct should be evaluated not only standing alone but, from the perspective of determining the punishable state of mind of the defendant, also in the context of the overwhelming evidence of its determination to withhold, mislead and deceive the public about the dangers of its product, thereby depriving the public of the opportunity to make a free and knowing decision about whether or not to smoke, how much to smoke and how difficult quitting smoking might be. Thus, as the jury found here, it is not for making a dangerous product that defendant should be punished. It is for concealing how dangerous the product is that R. J. Reynolds merits punishment.

Throughout this case the defendant vigorously proclaimed that smoking cigarettes is a choice, that people have been aware of its dangers for years, and that a person who smokes should be deemed to have assumed the risks associated with smoking. If Reynolds had made full disclosure, that argument would have great appeal in a free society. But, a free society where people are permitted to engage in conduct which may not always be beneficial or healthful to them depends on the manufacturers and purveyors of the products which people choose to consume being frank and open about the dangers of which they are aware in order to permit truly free choice. Here, the insidious nature of Reynolds' fraudulent concealment lies not only in the evidence of its bare failure to disclose vital information but also in the evidence of its campaign to obscure the public's ability to appreciate the risks of smoking by attacking the credibility of the public health community's concerns while at the same time withholding and ignoring evidence which was within its control that would have made the truth available to consumers. . . .

Concealment of the addictive nature of nicotine in the context of the knowledge by Reynolds of its health-related dangers, including specifically the causal relationship with PVD, brought with it a high likelihood at the time of the misconduct that serious harm would arise. Here, of course, serious harm—very foreseeable serious harm—occurred to Mr. Burton. He became addicted to a product which he consumed to the point that it caused him to so lose circulation in his legs that they both had to be amputated. This factor weighs heavily against Reynolds. It did not deceive him about facts which might affect the value of a luxury automobile, for example. It engaged in misconduct which consisted of specifically withholding information about how seriously harmful the product is to the persons of those enticed to use it. . . .

Reynolds is hugely profitable. Reynolds disclosed that it realized $505 million in net income in 2001, had over $1 billion in cash and cash equivalents and over $9 billion in stockholder equity. Plaintiff's expert testified that over the period from 1953 to 2001, Reynolds realized $34.6 billion in operating profit. While Reynolds presented expert testimony indicating that this figure was somewhat inflated because it included some profit from non-tobacco operations, an amount which Reynolds never quantified, and reflected operating profit instead of net income, there is no question that Reynolds reaped enormous profits from the sale of its cigarettes.

The court infers from the evidence that but for Reynold's misconduct, fewer people would have begun to smoke and those who had begun but desired to quit would have realized that the task might involve professional help. Knowledge that a product is not only risky to your health but also is addictive would seem to be a severe deterrent to consumption. The evidence does not permit a precise estimate of how many fewer cigarettes Reynolds would have sold had it been honest about the choice its potential consumers were asked to make. But, the vigor with which Reynolds pursued its campaign of concealment and obfuscation leads this court to the conclusion that the profitability of the misconduct was high....

The evidence does not reflect that Reynolds has repented of its ways. Its only grudging—and questionably sincere—concessions to the scientific evidence have been wrung from it through settlements of hotly contested lawsuits. It persists in its free choice mantra. Reynolds has not even said in any sincere and convincing fashion that it is sorry for what it did or for what happened to Mr. Burton. In many respects, this is the most disturbing aspect of this case and one which merits stiff punishment....

[T]he sheer magnitude of Reynolds' wealth makes it imperative that the award be in an amount which is high enough to have at least some impact in order to carry out the statutory purposes of punishment and deterrence....

In this case, the jury awarded compensatory damages in the amount of $198,400. Using this figure, a $15 million punitive damage award creates a ratio of approximately 75 to 1. The court believes that such a ratio is appropriate given the extremely reprehensible nature of Reynolds' conduct.... With all factors relevant to reprehensibility pointing toward a large award and because Mr. Burton suffered personal injury, where damages are not easily determined and translated into a dollar figure, the court concludes that a ratio of 75 to 1 is not constitutionally impermissible....

IT IS THEREFORE ORDERED that the Clerk of the Court shall modify and amend the judgment previously entered in this case to award plaintiff punitive damages in the amount of $15,000,000.

IT IS SO ORDERED

(continued from page 69)

The government has filed lawsuits, too.

Many suits filed against tobacco companies are filed by individuals, or are class-action lawsuits filed by groups of similarly situated individuals. But, in 1994, the state governments got into the act of suing "Big Tobacco."

In May 1994, the state of Mississippi became the first state to sue the tobacco industry to recover monies spent treating tobacco-caused illnesses. State Attorney General Mike Moore argued that the tobacco companies had committed conduct called "unjust enrichment" and should be forced to pay restitution to the state for its Medicaid costs due to tobacco-related illnesses. Law professor Howard Erichson writes that the government suits were a real breakthrough for two reasons: (1) state governments had the monetary resources to compete with the tobacco industry; and (2) the governmental suits avoided the classic argument advanced by the tobacco industry against individual smokers—individual responsibility. [10]

The lawsuits filed by Mississippi, Minnesota, and several other states led the tobacco companies to agree to an unprecedented agreement in 1998 called the Master Settlement Agreement. The gist was that the tobacco companies agreed to pay more than $200 billion to various states and to agree to stop marketing

A fter decades of futility in the courts, plaintiffs are now able to produce damning internal documents and witnesses against the tobacco giants and outraged juries are responding with punitive damages awards. Responses include last year's $3 billion punitive award in Piuze's prior cigarette case; $150 million in Portland, Oregon, in March; and a whopping $144 billion in a Florida class action in 2000. These numbers are huge, and some have been reduced by trial judges, but how can you find an appropriate punishment for these companies' evil, greedy, and deadly behavior?

—Mark Gottlieb of the Tobacco Products Liability Project

their products to children in order to avoid future lawsuits by the states.

———————————•————————————•————————————•———————————

For decades, large, wealthy tobacco companies have made billions of dollars from individual consumers by selling cancer-causing products. Tobacco companies have for years engaged in aggressive marketing campaigns encouraging the use of tobacco while concealing their full knowledge of the harmfulness and addictiveness of their products.

Tobacco companies should be subject to tort suits for their negligent and intentional conduct in the delivery of harmful products to the public. Although early tobacco suits may have laid much of the blame for people's health problems on individual responsibility, new evidence has shown just how addictive cigarettes are and how culpable the tobacco industry really was. These developments have led to recent large verdicts against Big Tobacco. If a jury believes that a tobacco manufacturer did engage in a pattern of deception, then it is likely to issue a large award to the plaintiff. Many of the large punitive damages awards made recently have been reduced on appeal. Still, the specter of liability remains a frightening possibility for the tobacco industry.

I believe they [the tobacco industry] are the most corrupt and evil corporate animal that has ever been created in this country's history. They sell a drug, they make a drug, and they sell it knowing that it's addictive. They market it to our children, who they know will become addicts and they know that they will die from causes attributable to tobacco-related disease.

—Mike Moore, Mississippi Attorney General

Suits Against Big Tobacco Ignore Personal Responsibility and Unfairly Demonize a Legal Activity

The price of one's freedom in a free society is responsibility for the consequences of one's actions. Liberty and responsibility are positively correlated. That's a fact. People who claim addiction causes people to smoke say the two are negatively correlated. That's fiction. We cannot increase freedom by decreasing personal responsibility. That's the road to serfdom.
— Jeffrey A. Schaler in "Smoking Right and Responsibility"

As cities across the United States continue to put public smoking bans into effect, some observers wonder what will happen to businesses that depended in various ways on tobacco. Not only have tobacco farmers and cigarette manufacturers suffered declines in profits, but smaller businesses, too, have begun to feel the effects. Bars and restaurants, in particular, where smoking was commonplace prior to the bans, have been hard hit. In September 2003, a report on New York City's smoking ban quoted restaurant owner Michelle Dell as saying,

"The smoking ban has devastated my business. I may have to lay off workers soon. We need help before it's too late."[1]

Virtually everyone knows that smoking is harmful. People know that it causes lung cancer. At least since the 1960s, people have been aware of the health risks of smoking. The Surgeon General in 1964 issued a warning that smoking was a health hazard. Decades of warnings on cigarette covers, public service announcements (many funded by the tobacco companies themselves), and warnings from the medical profession have told individuals of the harms. Nonetheless, in a free society, people have the right to choose whether or not to smoke.

Many juries reject plaintiffs' suits against Big Tobacco, reasoning that individuals know that cigarettes are harmful. Though the conduct of large tobacco companies has hardly been blameless, the companies do not force people to smoke. It is the individual who walks into a store and purchases the pack of cigarettes. "The campaign against cigarette manufacturers seeks to overturn the presumption of self-responsibility," writes one commentator. "What makes the case remarkable is that it potentially involves over a quarter of the total population of the U.S. and a product that has been legally sold for over 100 years."[2]

Many lawsuits against the tobacco industry claim that smokers' physical addiction to nicotine makes them smoke. They are powerless to quit. Jeffrey Schaler writes of the argument: "Tobacco caused them to smoke, they claim, as if tobacco had a will of its own. . . . This doublespeak contradicts the scientific evidence: smokers quit all the time—when it is important for them to do so."[3]

Tobacco companies have provided ample warning about the dangers of smoking.

Some courts have ruled that tobacco companies do not have a duty to warn individuals of the harms of smoking because

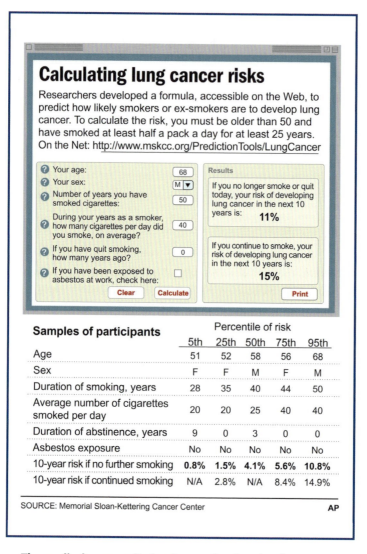

Calculating lung cancer risks

Researchers developed a formula, accessible on the Web, to predict how likely smokers or ex-smokers are to develop lung cancer. To calculate the risk, you must be older than 50 and have smoked at least half a pack a day for at least 25 years. On the Net: http://www.mskcc.org/PredictionTools/LungCancer

? Your age:	68	**Results**
? Your sex:	M ▼	If you no longer smoke or quit today, your risk of developing lung cancer in the next 10 years is: **11%**
? Number of years you have smoked cigarettes:	50	
? During your years as a smoker, how many cigarettes per day did you smoke, on average?	40	
? If you have quit smoking, how many years ago?	0	If you continue to smoke, your risk of developing lung cancer in the next 10 years is: **15%**
? If you have been exposed to asbestos at work, check here:	☐	

Clear   Calculate   Print

Samples of participants	Percentile of risk				
	5th	25th	50th	75th	95th
Age	51	52	58	56	68
Sex	F	F	M	F	M
Duration of smoking, years	28	35	40	44	50
Average number of cigarettes smoked per day	20	20	25	40	40
Duration of abstinence, years	9	0	3	0	0
Asbestos exposure	No	No	No	No	No
10-year risk if no further smoking	0.8%	1.5%	4.1%	5.6%	10.8%
10-year risk if continued smoking	N/A	2.8%	N/A	8.4%	14.9%

SOURCE: Memorial Sloan-Kettering Cancer Center   AP

The medical community has known for decades the many physical dangers associated with smoking. Even so, people—especially young people—often refuse to believe that they will suffer adverse effects from tobacco use. This chart provides a formula designed to calculate a person's risk of developing lung cancer, based on factors that include age, smoking habits, and exposure to asbestos.

smoking is an obvious health hazard. In *Gibbs* v. *Republic Tobacco, L.P.*, a federal district court in Florida rejected the claims of a man who alleged he had been harmed by loose-leaf tobacco products. The court wrote: "Courts throughout Florida have consistently and repeatedly held that there is no duty to warn consumers of the obvious dangers associated with certain products."[4] The court reasoned that the harm that may be caused by tobacco products was open and obvious.

A federal appeals court rejected the claim of a Tennessee man who sued a tobacco company after he contracted vascular disease. The man's doctors had testified that his cigarette smoking had caused the vascular disease. The man sued the tobacco company under the state's products liability statute. That law enables persons to sue for damages caused by "unreasonably dangerous" products. State law defined "unreasonably dangerous" as "dangerous to the extent beyond that which could be contemplated by the ordinary consumer who purchases it with the ordinary knowledge common to the community as to its characteristics." The court determined that cigarettes were not "unreasonably dangerous" because ordinary consumers should know of the risks and hazards. Tobacco has been used for more than four hundred years and "knowledge that cigarette smoking is harmful to health is widespread and can be considered part of the common knowledge of the community."[5]

Similarly, a federal court in Alabama rejected the products liability claims of a man in Alabama who sued a tobacco company for health problems engendered by his smoking. The court said, "Without question, the federally mandated warning on packages of cigarettes for the last thirty years has adequately warned the public of the dangers of tobacco smoking."[6]

Some courts have gone farther, reasoning that the risks of smoking have been known by consumers since 1950. In

Tompkins v. *R.J. Reynolds Tobacco Company*, a federal court in New York ruled that the tobacco company's expert witness had produced "overwhelming amounts of evidence showing a public awareness of the health risks of smoking since the turn of the twentieth century."[7] The court also questioned whether the plaintiff could show that the alleged failure of the tobacco company to warn the plaintiff of health hazards was the proximate, or legal, cause of his injuries when the plaintiff presented no evidence that he truly would have quit had he really known of the dangers associated with smoking.

In one case, a court rejected the claims of one person suing a tobacco company for the creation of a new tort called "intentional infliction of nicotine addiction." The court rejected the claim, stating that the plaintiff's attorney could not spell out the elements of such a novel cause of action when asked to do so in argument before the court. The plaintiff must provide notice to the defendant of the offense—"not a moving target," the court said.[8]

For example, a recent jury in Philadelphia rejected the claims of Lois Eiser, who sued the tobacco industry along with her now-deceased husband, William Eiser, a smoker who died of lung cancer. Eiser quit smoking in 1998 only after learning that he had lung cancer.

The plaintiff has a duty to prove causation.

A tort suit requires a plaintiff to prove (1) duty, (2) breach of duty, (3) causation, and (4) damages. The question of causation should cause juries to closely look at the plaintiff's own lifestyle and other bad habits. For instance, if a plaintiff died of heart disease, was it necessarily cigarette smoking that caused the death? The plaintiff may have had a family history of heart disease. He or she may also have had extreme stress from his or her job or personal life. The plaintiff could have had other bad habits that led to the disease. For example, if the plaintiff frequently ate fatty foods, that might just as easily have been the cause of the death.

Remember that a plaintiff has the burden of proof in a court case. The plaintiff must prove that the cigarette smoking was the proximate, or legal, cause of the plaintiff's harm. Many times, there can be multiple causes of a particular event. If there are several different causes, then tobacco companies should not be forced to take total responsibility for the person's unfortunate situation. The plaintiff must present clear medical proof that smoking itself was the major factor in the harm.

> • **What should a jury do if the plaintiff's condition was also caused by a heavy intake of unhealthy foods?**

Verdicts against tobacco show that the tort system is in danger.

The multimillion- or even multibillion-dollar verdicts against tobacco companies that have been imposed by some "runaway" juries shows the need for tort reform, according to some experts. They believe that the tobacco verdicts award large sums of money to persons whose harm was caused by their own bad choices.

> • **Should punitive damages be discontinued or limited? Does your state limit punitive damages by statute?**

One aspect of tort reform is limiting punitive damages. Punitive damages in tort law are damages designed to punish the wrongdoer. But tort reform advocates argue that punitive damages offer a windfall to undeserving plaintiffs and drive up the cost of doing business. The U.S. Supreme Court has twice in the last decade ruled that punitive damage awards can be so high as to shock the

FROM THE BENCH

BMW of North America, Inc. v. Gore, 517 U.S. 559 (1996)

"Elementary notions of fairness enshrined in our constitutional jurisprudence dictate that a person receive fair notice not only of the conduct that will subject him to punishment but also of the severity of the penalty that a State may impose."

Justice Stevens delivered the opinion of the Court.

In January 1990, Dr. Ira Gore, Jr. (respondent), purchased a black BMW sports sedan for $40,750.88 from an authorized BMW dealer in Birmingham, Alabama. After driving the car for approximately nine months, and without noticing any flaws in its appearance, Dr. Gore took the car to "Slick Finish," an independent detailer, to make it look "'snazzier than it normally would appear.'" 646 So. 2d 619, 621 (Ala. 1994). Mr. Slick, the proprietor, detected evidence that the car had been repainted. Convinced that he had been cheated, Dr. Gore brought suit against petitioner BMW of North America (BMW), the American distributor of BMW automobiles. Dr. Gore alleged . . . that the failure to disclose that the car had been repainted constituted suppression of a material fact. The complaint prayed for $500,000 in compensatory and punitive damages, and costs. . . .

Dr. Gore asserted that his repainted car was worthless than a car that had not been refinished. To prove his actual damages of $4,000, he relied on the testimony of a former BMW dealer, who estimated that the value of a repainted BMW was approximately 10 percent less than the value of a new car that had not been damaged and repaired. To support his claim for punitive damages, Dr. Gore introduced evidence that since 1983 BMW had sold 983 refinished cars as new, including 14 in Alabama, without disclosing that the cars had been repainted before sale at a cost of more than $300 per vehicle. Using the actual damage estimate of $4,000 per vehicle, Dr. Gore argued that a punitive award of $4 million would provide an appropriate penalty for selling approximately 1,000 cars for more than they were worth.

In defense of its disclosure policy, BMW argued that it was under no obligation to disclose repairs of minor damage to new cars and that Dr. Gore's car was as good as a car with the original factory finish. It disputed Dr. Gore's assertion that the value of the car was impaired by the repainting and argued that this good faith belief made a punitive award inappropriate. BMW also maintained that transactions in jurisdictions other than Alabama had no relevance to Dr. Gore's claim.

The jury returned a verdict finding BMW liable for compensatory damages of $4,000. In addition, the jury assessed $4 million in punitive damages, based on a determination that the nondisclosure policy constituted "gross, oppressive or malicious" fraud....

The Alabama Supreme Court did, however, rule in BMW's favor on one critical point: The court found that the jury improperly computed the amount of punitive damages by multiplying Dr. Gore's compensatory damages by the number of similar sales in other jurisdictions. Having found the verdict tainted, the court held that "a constitutionally reasonable punitive damages award in this case is $2,000,000."...

In our federal system, States necessarily have considerable flexibility in determining the level of punitive damages that they will allow in different classes of cases and in any particular case. Most States that authorize exemplary damages afford the jury similar latitude, requiring only that the damages awarded be reasonably necessary to vindicate the State's legitimate interests in punishment and deterrence. . . . Only when an award can fairly be categorized as "grossly excessive" in relation to these interests does it enter the zone of arbitrariness that violates the Due Process Clause of the Fourteenth Amendment....

Elementary notions of fairness enshrined in our constitutional jurisprudence dictate that a person receive fair notice not only of the conduct that will subject him to punishment but also of the severity of the penalty that a State may impose. Three guideposts, each of which indicates that BMW did not receive adequate notice of the magnitude of the sanction that Alabama might impose for adhering to the nondisclosure policy adopted in 1983, lead us to the conclusion that the $2 million award against BMW is grossly excessive: the degree of reprehensibility of the nondisclosure; the disparity between the harm or potential harm suffered by Dr. Gore and his punitive damages award; and the difference between this remedy and the civil penalties authorized or imposed in comparable cases....

That conduct is sufficiently reprehensible to give rise to tort liability, and even a modest award of exemplary damages, does not establish the high degree of culpability that warrants a substantial punitive damages award. Because this case exhibits none of the circumstances ordinarily associated with egregiously improper conduct, we are persuaded that BMW's conduct was not sufficiently reprehensible to warrant imposition of a $2 million exemplary damages award....

The judgment is reversed, and the case is remanded for further proceedings not inconsistent with this opinion.

It is so ordered.

conscience and violate the due process clause of the Fourteenth Amendment. In its 1996 decision *BMW of North America, Inc. v. Gore*, the U.S. Supreme Court vacated (set aside) a $2 million punitive damage award in a case with only a $4,000 compensatory damage award. A doctor had sued automobile manufacturer BMW after discovering that his vehicle had been repainted.

> • **Do you think someone should recover millions of dollars because his car had a faulty paint job? Where should juries draw the line when awarding punitive damages?**

In 2003, the U.S. Supreme Court vacated an even larger punitive damage award out of the state of Utah in *State Farm Mutual Auto Ins. Co. v. Campbell*.[9] In that case, the State Farm insurance company refused to settle a third-party claim on behalf of its insured. The insured, Chris Campbell, was sued for his role in an automobile accident. The other parties in the automobile accident agreed to settle the case for $50,000, but State Farm refused to settle, assuring Campbell that he would prevail at trial. Instead, the jury imposed liability on Campbell in the amount of $185,000. When Campbell sued State Farm, the jury awarded $1 million in compensatory damages, along with a whopping $145 million in punitive damages.

"A defendant should be punished for the conduct that harmed the plaintiff, not for being an unsavory individual or business," Justice Anthony Kennedy wrote for the U.S. Supreme Court. "Our jurisprudence and the principles it has now established demonstrate, however, that, in practice, few awards exceeding a single-digit ratio between punitive and compensatory damages, to a significant degree, will satisfy due process."[10] In other words, the Court said that rarely will a ratio exceeding ten to one in punitive to compensatory damages be constitutional. In the *Campbell* case, the ratio of punitive damages to compensatory damages was 145:1 and, therefore, too excessive, according to the Supreme Court.

The *Campbell* case has already had an effect on tobacco liability cases. For instance, on October 6, 2003, the U.S. Supreme Court set aside a punitive damage award against tobacco giant Philip Morris in the Oregon case of *Philip Morris U.S.A., Inc.*, v. *Williams*.[11] In the *Williams* case, an Oregon jury had awarded $79.5 million in punitive damages against Philip Morris on behalf of Mayola Williams, the widow of former smoker Jesse Williams. It is likely that, on remand, the punitive damage award will be reduced to conform to the earlier U.S. Supreme Court decisions in *Gore* and *Campbell*.

Traditionally, plaintiffs could not recover damages in

Synopsis of *Williams* v. *Philip Morris* (1997–present)

In October 2003, the U.S. Supreme Court vacated an $80 million verdict that had been brought by an Oregon state court against cigarette manufacturing company Philip Morris. The case had been brought to trial by the family of Jesse D. Williams, a janitor who died of lung cancer in 1997 after having smoked for some 40 years. His family claimed that the cigarette company had not made Williams aware that cigarette smoking was harmful, which encouraged him to continue to smoke. In its decision to throw out the original verdict, the Supreme Court ordered that the case be reviewed by lower courts to determine whether it was unconstitutionally excessive in the amount of damages awarded.

After hearing the case in 1999, an Oregon jury concluded that Philip Morris should pay the Williams family $79.5 million in punitive damages. Although the judge in the case, believing the amount excessive, reduced the number to $32 million, the state appeals court overruled the judge's decision and restored the punitive damages to the original amount. The Oregon supreme court declined to hear the tobacco company's appeal in December 2002. However, as indicated earlier, the U.S. Supreme Court may change that decision.

tort if they assumed the risk when they undertook a certain activity. Some observers believe that juries forget or ignore the doctrine of assumption of risk. Political commentator Walter Williams writes:

> As a result of the successful lawsuits against tobacco companies, assumption-of-risk doctrine is a skeleton of its past. For decades, under our traditional tort regime, if a plaintiff knows the risks of smoking, yet still smokes and contracts a tobacco-related illness, he had no claim against the tobacco manufacturer. That's all changed.[12]

Lawsuits against Big Tobacco create a slippery slope.

The suits against tobacco have led to a very bad precedent. Now, similar lawsuits have been filed against other harmful products, such as fatty fast foods. Already, several lawsuits have been filed against a number of fast-food restaurants, including McDonald's, Wendy's, Burger King, and Kentucky Fried Chicken. In one suit, a fifty-seven-year-old man who weighed 270 pounds sued various fast-food restaurants. He claimed that the restaurants had failed to warn him that a steady diet of fast food would lead to health problems, such as heart disease and diabetes.[13]

> • **Should fast-food companies be sued for their unhealthy products? Should they be required to issue health warnings, as tobacco companies do?**

Personal responsibility should guide the legal system's evaluation of suits against Big Tobacco. Even if the conduct of the tobacco giants was far less than admirable, the companies did not force people to smoke. Individuals had the freedom to choose. By imposing damages on tobacco companies, juries are punishing companies for the bad personal decisions of individuals.

> • **Should individuals assume the risk when they eat fatty foods or smoke cigarettes? Should anyone else be blamed if harm results from their behavior?**

Advertising Restrictions Against Tobacco Products Help Protect Children and Are Constitutional

Professional baseball player Honus Wagner, who played at the turn of the twentieth century, is rightfully remembered for his incredible hitting and skillful base-running. He may be better known today, however, for his stance against smoking.

In the early twentieth century, smoking was common and tobacco was advertised widely with limited restrictions. In fact, one common way to advertise tobacco was to give out baseball cards along with cigarettes and chewing tobacco. Like many ballplayers of the time, Pittsburgh Pirates shortstop Honus Wagner had his baseball card distributed with tobacco products. Wagner, himself a non-smoker, objected adamantly to this practice, believing that advertising tobacco products in a market geared toward children set a bad example for young people. In 1909, Wagner succeeded in getting his baseball card recalled. Interestingly, in the years since, the controversial card has become one of the most valuable of all time.

Commercial speech is not entitled to as much protection as other forms of speech.

Tobacco advertising is a form of commercial speech that implicates the First Amendment. However, the U.S. Supreme Court has declared that commercial speech is not entitled to as much protection as political and other forms of noncommercial speech. The Court has said that commercial speech receives less protection "commensurate with its subordinate position in the scale of First Amendment values."[1] The Court has recognized that there exists a "common-sense distinction between speech proposing a commercial transaction, which occurs in an area traditionally subject to government regulation, and other varieties of speech."[2]

Even when the U.S. Supreme Court extended a measure of First Amendment protection to commercial speech in 1976 in *Virginia State Board of Pharmacy* v. *Virginia Citizens Consumer Council, Inc.,* the justices still ruled that commercial speech was not entitled to full protection. The Court reasoned that commercial speech could be regulated more than political speech because it was "more easily verifiable" and "more durable."[3] The Court reasoned that the truthfulness about a price advertisement (commercial speech) could be determined more easily than a news report or political opinion. The Court also noted that commercial speech was less subject to being shut down because of its role in ensuring commercial profit.

> • **Should commercial speech be given less protection than political speech?**

In *Virginia Pharmacy*, the Court emphasized that deceptive, untruthful, and misleading commercial speech was entitled to no First Amendment protection. The tobacco companies have engaged in a pattern of deceptive and misleading advertising. For that reason, regulations on tobacco advertising do not violate freedom of speech.

A few years after the *Virginia Pharmacy* case, the Supreme Court established a balancing test that provided less constitutional protection for commercial speech than under *Virginia Pharmacy*. In *Central Hudson Gas & Electric*

FROM THE BENCH

Virginia State Board of Pharmacy v. Virginia Citizens Consumer Council, Inc., 425 U.S. 748 (1976)

The plaintiff-appellees in this case attack, as violative of the First and Fourteenth Amendments, [note 1] that portion of § 54-524.35 of Va. Code Ann. (1974), which provides that a pharmacist licensed in Virginia is guilty of unprofessional [750] conduct if he "(3) publishes, advertises or promotes, directly or indirectly, in any manner whatsoever, any amount, price, fee, premium, discount, rebate or credit terms . . . for any drugs which may be dispensed only by prescription." The three-judge District Court declared the quoted portion of the statute "void and of no effect," Jurisdictional Statement, App. 1, and enjoined the defendant-appellants, the Virginia State Board of Pharmacy and the individual members of that Board, from enforcing it. 373 F. Supp. 683 (ED Va. 1974). . . .

Since the challenged restraint is one that peculiarly concerns the licensed pharmacist in Virginia, we begin with a description of that profession as it exists under Virginia law.

The regulatory body is the appellant Virginia State Board of Pharmacy. The Board is broadly charged by statute with various responsibilities, including the "[m]aintenance of the quality, quantity, integrity, safety and efficacy of drugs or devices distributed, dispensed or administered." . . .

Inasmuch as only a licensed pharmacist may dispense prescription drugs in

Corp. v. *Public Service Commission of N.Y.*, the Court ruled that restrictions on commercial speech have to meet a less burdensome standard:

1. the speech must concern lawful activity and not be misleading;

2. the asserted governmental interest must be substantial;

3. the regulation must directly and materially advance the governmental interest;

Virginia, advertising or other affirmative dissemination of prescription drug price information is effectively forbidden in the State....

The question first arises whether, even assuming that First Amendment protection attaches to the flow of drug price information, it is a protection enjoyed by the appellees as recipients of the information, and not solely, if at all, by the advertisers themselves who seek to disseminate that information....

The appellants contend that the advertisement of prescription drug prices is outside the protection of the First Amendment because it is "commercial speech."...

[T]he Court has never denied protection on the ground that the speech in issue was "commercial speech."...

If there is a kind of commercial speech that lacks all First Amendment protection, therefore, it must be distinguished by its content....

Untruthful speech, commercial or otherwise, has never been protected for its own sake. Obviously, much commercial speech is not provably false, or even wholly false, but only deceptive or misleading. We foresee no obstacle to a State's dealing effectively with this problem. The First Amendment, as we construe it today, does not prohibit the State from insuring that the stream of commercial information flow cleanly as well as freely....

What is at issue is whether a State may completely suppress the dissemination of concededly truthful information about entirely lawful activity, fearful of that information's effect upon its disseminators and its recipients. Reserving other questions, we conclude that the answer to this one is in the negative.

4. the regulation must be no more extensive than necessary to further the governmental interest.[4]

When applying the *Central Hudson* test to tobacco ad regulations, many regulations survive judicial review. First, it is highly possible that many tobacco ads are misleading and deceptive. Second, the government surely has a substantial, if not compelling, interest in protecting minors from underage smoking. The question becomes whether the regulations directly advance the governmental interests and whether they are too broad.

The electronic ban on cigarette advertising is necessary.

The federal courts have upheld federal bans on radio and television advertisements of cigarettes. Section 6 of the Public Health Cigarette Smoking Act of 1969 provided: "It shall be unlawful to advertise cigarettes on any medium of electronic communication subject to the jurisdiction of the Federal Communications Commission."

Several corporations operating radio stations challenged the law on First Amendment free speech grounds and Fifth Amendment due process grounds. They argued that the ban violated the First Amendment because it prevented them from communicating about their products on an important medium. They claimed that the ban violated their Fifth Amendment rights because the classification between the broadcast medium and the print medium with regard to cigarettes was arbitrary and irrational. Due process requires that legislation have a rational basis and not be arbitrary.

In *Capital Broadcasting Co.* v. *Mitchell*, a panel of three federal judges ruled 2–1 that the ban was constitutional. The majority rejected the First Amendment argument, noting that the corporations "have lost no right to speak—only an ability to collect revenue from others for broadcasting their commercial messages." The court ruled that the radio stations could air their own point of view about the smoking controversy. The majority also rejected the Fifth Amendment argument, finding there was a rational basis to treat the broadcast medium differently from the print medium. "Substantial evidence showed that the most persuasive advertising was being conducted on radio and television, and that these broadcasts were particularly effective in reaching a very large audience of young people," the majority wrote.[5]

> • Was this case rightly decided? Does the electronic ban on cigarettes violate the First Amendment right of free speech?

Tobacco companies have targeted children.

Cigarette companies aimed their advertising at specific groups,

FROM THE BENCH

Capital Broadcasting Co. v. *Mitchell*, 333 F.Supp. 582, 586 (D.D.C. 1971)

Substantial evidence showed that the most persuasive advertising was being conducted on radio and television, and that these broadcasts were particularly effective in reaching a very large audience of young people.

Thus, Congress knew of the close relationship between cigarette commercials broadcast on the electronic media and their potential influence on young people, and was no doubt aware that the younger the individual, the greater the reliance on the broadcast message rather than the written word.

A pre-school or early elementary school age child can hear and understand a radio commercial or see, hear and understand a television commercial, while at the same time be substantially unaffected by an advertisement printed in a newspaper, magazine or appearing on a billboard.

including minorities and children. "But it's children that the tobacco companies' advertising affects most of all," comedian Steve Allen wrote in his book, *The Passionate Nonsmoker's Bill of Rights.*[6]

For years, the cartoon "Joe Camel" and the cowboy figure "The Marlboro Man" were used to depict the tobacco industry in a positive light. The Joe Camel character was popular and well known among teenagers. One study by the *Journal of the American Medical Association* showed that 93 percent of high school students knew which cigarette brand was promoted by "Joe Camel," as compared with 58 percent of adults. In the same findings, 43 percent of the students thought "Joe Camel" was "cool," as compared with 26 percent of adults.[7]

The government has a substantial, even compelling, interest in preventing minors from smoking. The government must have broad powers to reduce youth smoking, which is illegal. Unfortunately, tobacco companies have long been engaged in a pattern of targeting young people in an effort to attract new smokers. Plaintiffs in one case against the tobacco companies produced an internal memo from a smoking executive stating: "[T]here is certainly nothing immoral or unethical about our Company attempting to attract [underage] smokers to our products." The executive also urged the company to develop new products to influence "pre-smokers to try smoking, learn to smoke and become confirmed smokers."[8]

• **Was Joe Camel an attempt to target kids as smokers?**

U.S. Senator Edward Kennedy (D-MA) writes that the tobacco companies continue to market aggressively to children:

> Contrary to industry claims, the major tobacco companies
> have not abandoned their aggressive marketing strategy

aimed at children. The Master Settlement Agreement (MSA) entered into between the major tobacco companies and forty-six states in 1998 contained an industry promise not to take any action, directly or indirectly, to target youth. Within months of making that commitment, the industry massively increased the amount it spent on marketing. . . . Much of the spending increase has been on marketing that is known to appeal to youths. A March 2002 survey found that while only twenty-seven percent of adults had seen tobacco advertisements in the preceding two weeks, sixty-four percent of teenagers recalled seeing tobacco ads during that period. The industry is still promoting cigarettes in the ways most likely to reach children.[9]

The American Heart Association says that studies show tobacco companies increased their advertising in youth magazines after the signing of the Master Settlement Agreement. A 2001 study in the *New England Journal of Medicine* concluded that the Master Settlement Agreement has had little, if any, effect on youth exposure to cigarette ads.[10] The Department of Health and Human Services estimates that the vast majority of smokers, up to 90 percent, begin to smoke when they are twenty years of age or younger.[11]

Much of the impetus for the 1998 Master Settlement Agreement was a desire to prevent tobacco companies from advertising in venues popular among young people. In California, the state attorney general sued tobacco giant R.J. Reynolds for violating the Master Settlement Agreement by placing ads in magazines with a heavy youth readership, including *Sports Illustrated*, *Spin*, and *Hot Rod* magazines. A trial judge agreed and fined R.J. Reynolds $20 million. The judge ordered the tobacco corporation to "reduce youth exposure" to cigarette ads.

Tobacco companies have targeted minority communities.

The Surgeon General has reported that the tobacco industry has engaged in a pattern of targeting certain minority communities. Some of the Surgeon General's findings include:

- Studies have found a higher density of tobacco billboards in racial/ethnic minority communities. For example, a 1993 study in San Diego, California, found that the highest proportion of tobacco billboards were posted in Asian-American communities and the lowest proportion were in white communities.

- The tobacco industry commonly uses cultural symbols and designs to target racial/ethnic populations. American Spirit cigarettes were promoted as "natural" cigarettes; the package featured an American Indian smoking a pipe. In addition, certain tobacco product advertisements have used visual images, such as American Indian warriors, to target their products.

- A one-year study found that three major African-American publications—*Ebony*, *Jet*, and *Essence*—received proportionately higher profits from cigarette advertisements than did other magazines.[12]

> • **Should there be a law against targeted advertising by race? How might such a law affect other products and industries?**

Law professor Vernellia R. Randall writes: "The tobacco industry specifically targeted the African-American community with their product. It disproportionately flooded the African-American community with advertisement and cigarettes. It promoted a more addicting drug in the African-American community. As a result, more African-American adults smoke, are more addicted, and have greater illness due to smoking."[13]

The tobacco companies developed specially named brands targeting African Americans. "To say that the black community has been overrun with tobacco advertising is an understatement," Professor Randall writes. "The size and number of billboards in minority communities have created an intrusive and persistent form of advertising. There is absolutely no way to avoid it."[14]

Several studies have shown that many minority communities are deluged with billboards of tobacco and alcohol products. The Centers for Disease Control and Prevention has said that tobacco billboards appear at a rate four to five times greater in minority neighborhoods than in other neighborhoods.

The tobacco companies gave up many of their free speech rights in the Master Settlement Agreement.

Even if the First Amendment did allow tobacco companies to advertise truthfully about their products, the tobacco companies relinquished many of their free speech rights when they agreed to the historic 1998 Master Settlement Agreement. In November 23, 1998, officials from forty-six states, the District of Columbia, Puerto Rico, the U.S. Virgin Islands, and other U.S. territories made an agreement with the five largest tobacco manufacturers: Brown & Williamson, Lorillard Tobacco Company, Philip Morris, R.J. Reynolds Tobacco Company, and Liggett & Myers.

Four states—Florida, Minnesota, Mississippi, and Texas—had already settled with the tobacco companies for $40 billion. As part of the agreement, the companies agreed to pay more than $200 billion to the states for the next twenty-five years. In addition, the tobacco companies agreed to a whole host of advertising restrictions. Many of these restrictions involve advertising in places likely to be frequented by children. They include banning cartoon characters in tobacco ads, such as Joe Camel; banning outdoor tobacco advertising; banning the use of tobacco brand names at stadiums and arenas; banning distribution and sale of non-tobacco merchandise with brand-name logos (such as caps and T-shirts); and banning cigarette brands from being named after recognized non-tobacco brand names or trade names, recognized sports teams, entertainment groups, or celebrities. The agreement also calls for the removal of tobacco billboards.

> • **Is the Master Settlement Agreement a good idea? Why or why not?**

Restrictions on tobacco advertising are necessary in light of the industries' continued and relentless marketing campaigns. Study after study has established that the tobacco companies have targeted their marketing to minorities, women, and especially children. Even after the 1998 Master Settlement Agreement, some evidence suggests that the tobacco companies are still targeting new smokers who are underage. Recent lawsuits in Arizona, California, and elsewhere establish that various tobacco companies are not adhering to the Master Settlement Agreement.

Even though the U.S. Supreme Court has given more protection to commercial speech in recent years, the Court still recognizes that government has more control over commercial speech than noncommercial speech. The distinction between commercial and noncommercial speech has stood since modern commercial speech doctrine was first defined in the mid-1970s. It also should not be forgotten that the tobacco companies agreed to many self-imposed restrictions on tobacco advertising in their contract with the states.

Tobacco Advertising Is a Form of Protected Speech

For decades, the name "Winston-Salem"—the North Carolina town that is home to the R.J. Reynolds Tobacco Company—was almost synonymous with stock-car racing and NASCAR (the National Association for Stock Car Auto Racing). The tobacco giant had sponsored the famous Winston Racing Series for twenty-six years, providing regional and national prizes to drivers that totaled some $1.4 million each year.

The long-term relationship between tobacco and racing came to a dramatic end in 1999, however. In response to the ever-growing controversy over smoking and particularly the influence of tobacco advertisements on young people, R.J. Reynolds decided to withdraw its sponsorship of the Winston Racing Series. As part of the company's reason for the decision was the fact that in some places, NASCAR drivers are only sixteen to seventeen years old (under the legal age for using tobacco products), and would therefore be among the age group to which cigarette companies are not permitted to advertise under the constraints of the Master Settlement Agreement. Many racing fans were upset over the decision, fearing NASCAR would suffer financial setbacks and decrying the end of a tradition.

Advertising—like R.J. Reynolds's former sponsorship of NASCAR—remains an important part of our consumer culture. The First Amendment provides a substantial degree of protection for advertising about legal products. And, unpopular as it may be, tobacco is a legal product for adults. For many years, advertising received no First Amendment protection. But, in the mid-1970s, the U.S. Supreme Court recognized that a consumer's interest in the free flow of commercial information was important enough to merit protection.

In its 1976 decision *Virginia State Board of Pharmacy* v. *Virginia Citizens Consumer Council, Inc.,* the Supreme Court created the commercial speech doctrine and explicitly ruled that advertising was entitled to First Amendment protection.[1] The Court recognized that the public had the right to receive information and ideas. It also determined that individuals have the right to receive the free flow of commercial information.

Even before the Supreme Court explicitly protected commercial speech under the umbrella of the First Amendment, some judges recognized that suppression of information about the smoking controversy violated freedom of speech. In the *Capital Broadcasting Co.* v. *Mitchell* case discussed in the previous chapter, Judge Skelly Wright dissented from the panel majority.

"It would be difficult to argue that there are many who mourn for the Marlboro Man or miss the ungrammatical Winston jingles," he wrote. "Moreover, overwhelming scientific evidence makes plain that the Salem girl was in fact a seductive merchant of death—that the real 'Marlboro Country' is the graveyard. But the First Amendment does not protect only speech that is healthy or harmless."[2] Wright reasoned that the theory behind the First Amendment is based on the belief that people will make the right choice if they are presented with all points of views on controversial topics.[3]

• **Did Judge Wright have a valid argument?**

FROM THE BENCH

Virginia State Board of Pharmacy v. Virginia Citizens Consumer Council, Inc., 425 U.S. 748, 765 (1976)

Generalizing, society also may have a strong interest in the free flow of commercial information. Even an individual advertisement, though entirely "commercial," may be of general public interest.... Obviously, not all commercial messages contain the same or even a very great public interest element. There are few to which such an element, however, could not be added. Our pharmacist, for example, could cast himself as a commentator on store-to-store disparities in drug prices, giving his own and those of a competitor as proof. We see little point in requiring him to do so, and little difference if he does not.

Moreover, there is another consideration that suggests that no line between publicly "interesting" or "important" commercial advertising and the opposite kind could ever be drawn. Advertising, however tasteless and excessive it sometimes may seem, is nonetheless dissemination of information as to who is producing and selling what product, for what reason, and at what price. So long as we preserve a predominantly free enterprise economy, the allocation of our resources in large measure will be made through numerous private economic decisions. It is a matter of public interest that those decisions, in the aggregate, be intelligent and well informed. To this end, the free flow of commercial information is indispensable. And if it is indispensable to the proper allocation of resources in a free enterprise system, it is also indispensable to the formation of intelligent opinions as to how that system ought to be regulated or altered. Therefore, even if the First Amendment were thought to be primarily an instrument to enlighten public decisionmaking in a democracy, we could not say that the free flow of information does not serve that goal.

Commercial speech deserves greater protection.

In the mid-1990s, the U.S. Supreme Court granted commercial speech even more protection, particularly in cases involving alcohol, gambling, and tobacco products. In *Rubin* v. *Coors Brewing Company,* the Court unanimously struck down a regulation of the Federal Alcohol Administration Act prohibiting the display of alcoholic content on beer labels.[4] The next year, in *44 Liquormart, Inc.* v. *Rhode Island*, the Supreme Court struck down two Rhode Island laws that prohibited advertising the retail prices of alcoholic beverages. The state argued that the ban was necessary to reduce alcohol consumption.[5] The Court ruled that the state's ban violated the First Amendment. In a concurring opinion, Justice Clarence Thomas went so far as to call for the abandonment of the distinction between commercial and noncommercial speech: "I do not see a philosophical or historical basis for asserting that commercial speech is of lower value than noncommercial speech. Indeed, some historical materials suggest to the contrary."[6] These decisions set the stage for the Court's decision in a tobacco advertisement case.

> • **Do you agree with Justice Thomas's views on commercial speech?**

The *Lorillard* decision upholds some commercial speech rights in regard to tobacco.

In *Lorillard Tobacco Co.* v. *Reilly*, the Supreme Court examined the constitutionality of several parts of a Massachusetts law designed to limit the advertising of tobacco products in the state. The attorney of the state argued that the state law was necessary to "close holes" in the Master Settlement Agreement signed by forty-six states and five major tobacco manufacturers.

The law prohibited outdoor advertising and "point-of-sale" advertising of tobacco products in the state. It applied to cigarettes, cigars, and smokeless tobacco. It defined outdoor advertising as follows:

> Outdoor advertising, including advertising in enclosed stadiums and advertising from within a retail establishment that is directed toward or visible from the outside of the establishment, in any location that is within a 1,000 foot radius of any public playground, playground area in a public park, elementary school or secondary school.

It also defined point-of-sale advertising:

> Point of sale advertising of cigarettes or smokeless tobacco products any portion of which is placed lower than five feet from the floor of any retail establishment which is located within a one thousand foot radius of any public playground, playground area in a public park, elementary school or secondary school, and which is not an adult-only retail establishment.

The Supreme Court first ruled that the state advertising restrictions as applied to cigarettes was preempted, or trumped, by a federal law known as the Federal Cigarette Labeling and Advertising Act (FCLAA). One provision of the FCLAA provided that "no requirement or prohibition based on smoking and health shall be imposed under State law with respect to the advertising or promotion of any cigarettes the packages of which are labeled in conformity with the provisions of this chapter."[7]

The tobacco companies argued that this provision of federal law means that the Massachusetts law regulating cigarette advertising was unconstitutional because it infringed on an area of exclusive federal domain. The state argued that the federal law did not preempt its law because the federal law only preempted state laws dealing with the content of tobacco advertising.

(continued on page 106)

FROM THE BENCH

Lorillard Tobacco Co. v. Reilly, 533 U.S. 525 (2001).

Justice O'Connor delivered the opinion of the Court.

In January 1999, the Attorney General of Massachusetts promulgated comprehensive regulations governing the advertising and sale of cigarettes, smokeless tobacco, and cigars. Petitioners, a group of cigarette, smokeless tobacco, and cigar manufacturers and retailers, filed suit in Federal District Court claiming that the regulations violate federal law and the United States Constitution. The first question presented for our review is whether certain cigarette advertising regulations are pre-empted by the Federal Cigarette Labeling and Advertising Act (FCLAA). The second question presented is whether certain regulations governing the advertising and sale of tobacco products violate the First Amendment.

In November 1998, Massachusetts, along with over 40 other States, reached a land-mark agreement with major manufacturers in the cigarette industry. The signatory States settled their claims against these companies in exchange for monetary payments and permanent injunctive relief. At the press conference covering Massachusetts' decision to sign the agreement, then-Attorney General Scott Harshbarger announced that as one of his last acts in office, he would create consumer protection regulations to restrict advertising and sales practices for tobacco products. He explained that the regulations were necessary in order to "close holes" in the settlement agreement and "to stop Big Tobacco from recruiting new customers among the children of Massachusetts."

In January 1999, pursuant to his authority to prevent unfair or deceptive practices in trade, Mass. Gen. Laws, ch. 93A, §2 (1997), the Massachusetts Attorney General (Attorney General) promulgated regulations governing the sale and advertisement of cigarettes, smokeless tobacco, and cigars. The purpose of the cigarette and smokeless tobacco regulations is "to eliminate deception and unfairness in the way cigarettes and smokeless tobacco products are marketed, sold and distributed in Massachusetts in order to address the incidence of cigarette smoking and smokeless tobacco use by children under legal age . . . [and] in order to prevent access to such products by underage consumers. . . ." The regulations have a broader scope than the master settlement agreement, reaching advertising, sales practices, and members of the tobacco industry not covered by the agreement. The regulations place a variety of restrictions on outdoor advertising, point-of-sale advertising, retail sales transactions, transactions by mail, promotions, sampling of products, and labels for cigars. . . .

Before the effective date of the regulations, February 1, 2000, members of the tobacco industry sued the Attorney General in the United States District Court for the District of Massachusetts [claiming] that many of the regulations violate the Commerce Clause, the Supremacy Clause, the First and Fourteenth Amendments....

For over 25 years, the Court has recognized that commercial speech does not fall outside the purview of the First Amendment. Instead, the Court has afforded commercial speech a measure of First Amendment protection " 'commensurate' " with its position in relation to other constitutionally guaranteed expression. In recognition of the "distinction between speech proposing a commercial trans-action, which occurs in an area traditionally subject to government regulation, and other varieties of speech," we developed a framework for analyzing regulations of commercial speech that is "substantially similar" to the test for time, place, and manner restrictions. The analysis contains four elements: "At the outset, we must determine whether the expression is protected by the First Amendment. For commercial speech to come within that provision, it at least must concern lawful activity and not be misleading. Next, we ask whether the asserted governmental interest is substantial. If both inquiries yield positive answers, we must determine whether the regulation directly advances the governmental interest asserted, and whether it is not more extensive than is necessary to serve that interest.".....

The Attorney General has assumed for purposes of summary judgment that petitioners' speech is entitled to First Amendment protection. With respect to the second step, none of the petitioners contests the importance of the State's interest in preventing the use of tobacco products by minors....

The Attorney General relies in part on evidence gathered by the Food and Drug Administration (FDA) in its attempt to regulate the advertising of cigarettes and smokeless tobacco. The FDA promulgated the advertising regulations after finding that the period prior to adulthood is when an overwhelming majority of Americans first decide to use tobacco products, and that advertising plays a crucial role in that decision. We later held that the FDA lacks statutory authority to regulate tobacco products. Nevertheless, the Attorney General relies on the FDA's proceedings and other studies to support his decision that advertising affects demand for tobacco products.

In its rulemaking proceeding, the FDA considered several studies of tobacco adver-tising and trends in the use of various tobacco products. The Surgeon General's report and the Institute of Medicine's report found that "there is sufficient evidence to con-clude that advertising and labeling play a significant and important contributory role in a young person's decision to use cigarettes or smokeless tobacco products."...

The State's interest in preventing underage tobacco use is substantial, and even compelling, but it is no less true that the sale and use of tobacco products by adults is a legal activity. We must consider that tobacco retailers and manufacturers have an interest in conveying truthful information about their products to adults, and adults have a corresponding interest in receiving truthful information about tobacco products. In a case involving indecent speech on the Internet we explained that "the governmental interest in protecting children from harmful materials . . . does not justify an unnecessarily broad suppression of speech addressed to adults." As the State protects children from tobacco advertisements, tobacco manufacturers and retailers and their adult consumers still have a protected interest in communication.

In some instances, Massachusetts' outdoor advertising regulations would impose particularly onerous burdens on speech. . . . If some retailers have relatively small advertising budgets, and use few avenues of communication, then the Attorney General's outdoor advertising regulations potentially place a greater, not lesser, burden on those retailers' speech. . . .

We conclude that the Attorney General has failed to show that the outdoor advertising regulations for smokeless tobacco and cigars are not more extensive than necessary to advance the State's substantial interest in preventing underage tobacco use. . . .

We have observed that "tobacco use, particularly among children and adolescents, poses perhaps the single most significant threat to public health in the United States." From a policy perspective, it is understandable for the States to attempt to prevent minors from using tobacco products before they reach an age where they are capable of weighing for themselves the risks and potential benefits of tobacco use, and other adult activities. Federal law, however, places limits on policy choices available to the States.

In this case, Congress enacted a comprehensive scheme to address cigarette smoking and health in advertising and pre-empted state regulation of cigarette advertising that attempts to address that same concern, even with respect to youth. The First Amendment also constrains state efforts to limit advertising of tobacco products, because so long as the sale and use of tobacco is lawful for adults, the tobacco industry has a protected interest in communicating information about its products and adult customers have an interest in receiving that information.

To the extent that federal law and the First Amendment do not prohibit state action, States and localities remain free to combat the problem of underage tobacco use by appropriate means. . . .

(continued from page 102)

Because its law was purely a locational restriction, the state argued that FCLAA had no effect upon it.

The Supreme Court disagreed, writing that "a distinction between state regulation of the location as opposed to the content of cigarette advertising has no foundation in the text of the preemption provision."[8]

The Court then examined whether the outdoor advertising and point-of-sale bans on cigars and smokeless tobacco products violated the First Amendment. The Court determined that the state attorney general had a substantial, even compelling, interest in protecting minors from tobacco products. But it decided that the one-thousand-foot restriction on outdoor advertising was simply too broad. "In some geographical areas, these regulations would constitute nearly a complete ban on the communication of truthful information about smokeless tobacco and cigars to adult consumers," the Court wrote.[9]

"The State's interest in preventing underage tobacco use is substantial, and even compelling, but it is by no means less true that the sale and use of tobacco products by adults is a legal activity," the Court added. Citing a case about the restriction of indecent speech on the Internet, the Court emphasized that the government cannot use the protection of minors as a means to suppress the free speech rights of adults.[10]

The Court emphasized that the one-thousand-foot ban on outdoor advertising was particularly onerous because the law's definition of outdoor advertising included advertising in stores if the ad were visible from outside the store.

The justices also focused on the fact that the regulations would restrict the free speech rights of adults. Even though the state has a substantial interest in protecting minors from tobacco usage, tobacco manufacturers and adult consumers have a First Amendment right to provide and receive information about lawful products.

The Court also struck down the point-of-sale provision prohibiting advertising fewer than five feet from the floor of retail advertisements. The majority determined that this restriction did not advance the state's goals in protecting minors. "Not all children are less than 5 feet tall, and those who are certainly have the ability to look up and take in their surroundings."[11]

Justice Clarence Thomas wrote separately to emphasize his oft-stated view that commercial speech, including tobacco advertising, should not receive second-class status in First Amendment jurisprudence.

The state of Massachusetts could have used other means to try to prevent underage tobacco smoking. These means would not have violated the First Amendment. The state could have more vigorously enforced its existing laws prohibiting the sale of tobacco to minors. The state could have financed its own antitobacco messages or the state could have initiated youth programs designed to warn about the dangers of smoking.[12]

Even the justices who dissented on the preemption issue

FROM THE BENCH

Justice Clarence Thomas's Concurring Opinion in *Lorillard Tobacco Co. v. Reilly*, 533 U.S. 525 (2001).

No legislature has ever sought to restrict speech about an activity it regarded as harmless and inoffensive. Calls for limits on expression always are made when the specter of some threatened harm is looming. The identity of the harm may vary. People will be inspired by totalitarian dogmas and subvert the Republic. They will be inflamed by racial demagoguery and embrace hatred and bigotry. Or they will be enticed by cigarette advertisements and choose to smoke, risking disease. It is therefore no answer for the State to say that the makers of cigarettes are doing harm: perhaps they are. But in that respect they are no different from the purveyors of other harmful products, or the advocates of harmful ideas. When the State seeks to silence them, they are all entitled to the protection of the First Amendment.

were troubled by the outdoor advertising regulations. In his dissent, Justice John Paul Stevens said that he would favor sending the case down to the lower court for the development of further evidence on the breadth of the regulation.

One legal commentator has written that the *Lorillard* decision

> effectively places advertising on the same constitutional level as advertising for other lawful goods and services under the First Amendment and creates a strong likelihood that laws restricting the flow of protected commercial speech in order to manipulate consumer behavior are likely to be struck down as unconstitutional despite a compelling regulatory interest such as protecting the health of minors.[13]

The Master Settlement Agreement was unconstitutional and set a bad precedent.

In the 1998 Master Settlement Agreement entered into by the largest tobacco companies and forty-six states, the tobacco industry voluntarily agreed to abide by a series of advertising restrictions and to pay billions of dollars in damages to the states.

The restrictions on advertising in the Master Settlement Agreement are onerous. They include:

- Tobacco ads are limited to black-and-white backgrounds except for "adult-only facilities" and "adult publications."

- Tobacco companies cannot use cartoon characters, such as Joe Camel, to advertise their products.

- Tobacco companies cannot target youth in the advertising, promotion, or marketing of tobacco products.

- Tobacco companies cannot sponsor concerts or other events with significant youth audiences, including team sporting events, such as football games.

- Tobacco brand names cannot be advertised at stadiums and arenas.

- Tobacco outdoor advertising is banned, including billboards, signs, and placards larger than a poster.

- Tobacco companies cannot pay entertainment executives to promote tobacco products in television shows, movies, live performances, and video games.

> • **Why would the tobacco companies agree to all of these restrictions? If these restrictions were in a law, would they violate the First Amendment?**

Legal experts have noted that many of these advertising restrictions in the Master Settlement Agreement would not hold water if they were passed by a legislative body and challenged in court. "Many of the restrictions on advertising included in the settlement agreement could not be imposed legislatively because they would violate the First Amendment," says Richard Samp, chief counsel of the Washington Legal Foundation.[14]

Others point out the Master Settlement Agreement presents other constitutional problems aside from the First Amendment. Lawyer Margaret Little writes: "The MSA is extra-constitutional legislation crafted outside of any statehouse or Congress in disregard of the structural constitutions it displaces, and it constitutes bad public policy and worse precedent."[15]

Tobacco is unquestionably a harmful product, but in American society, it is still legal. The U.S. Supreme Court has established that the First Amendment provides in a free society that consumers can make their own choices and that the government cannot suppress truthful speech even about harmful products. Under the Court's commercial speech doctrine,

Excerpts from Master Settlement Agreement, 1998

WHEREAS, more than 40 States have commenced litigation asserting various claims for monetary, equitable and injunctive relief against certain tobacco product manufacturers and others as defendants, and the States that have not filed suit can potentially assert similar claims; ...

WHEREAS, defendants have denied each and every one of the Settling States' allegations of unlawful conduct or wrongdoing and have asserted a number of defenses to the Settling States' claims, which defenses have been contested by the Settling States;

WHEREAS, the Settling States and the Participating Manufacturers are committed to reducing underage tobacco use by discouraging such use and by preventing Youth access to Tobacco Products ...

NOW, THEREFORE, BE IT KNOWN THAT, in consideration of the implementation of tobacco-related health measures and the payments to be made by the Participating Manufacturers, the release and discharge of all claims by the Settling States, and such other consideration as described herein, the sufficiency of which is hereby acknowledged, the Settling States and the Participating Manufacturers, acting by and through their authorized agents, memorialize and agree as follows: ...

III. Permanent Relief

(a) *Prohibition on Youth Targeting.* No Participating Manufacturer may take any action, directly or indirectly, to target Youth within any Settling State in the advertising, promotion or marketing of Tobacco Products, or take any action the primary purpose of which is to initiate, maintain or increase the incidence of Youth smoking within any Settling State.

the government can only restrict truthful commercial speech if it shows that its regulations directly advance and further substantial governmental interests. Furthermore, the government cannot use a protection-of-minors rationale to restrict the free speech rights of adults. The basic theory behind the First Amendment is that the government cannot suppress speech, particularly truthful speech about lawful products and issues of public importance.

(b) *Ban on Use of Cartoons.* Beginning 180 days after the MSA Execution Date, no Participating Manufacturer may use or cause to be used any Cartoon in the advertising, promoting, packaging or labeling of Tobacco Products.

(c) *Limitation of Tobacco Brand Name Sponsorships.*

(1) *Prohibited Sponsorships.* After the MSA Execution Date, no Participating Manufacturer may engage in any Brand Name Sponsorship in any State consisting of:

(A) concerts; or

(B) events in which the intended audience is comprised of a significant percentage of Youth; or

(C) events in which any paid participants or contestants are Youth; or

(D) any athletic event between opposing teams in any football, basketball, baseball, soccer or hockey league ...

(3) *Related Sponsorship Restrictions.* With respect to any Brand Name Sponsorship permitted under this subsection (c):

(A) advertising of the Brand Name Sponsorship event shall not advertise any Tobacco Product (other than the Brand Name to identify such Brand Name Sponsorship event);

(B) no Participating Manufacturer may refer to a Brand Name Sponsorship event or to a celebrity or other person in such an event in its advertising of a Tobacco Product....

Conclusion

More than twenty years ago, Judge Skelly Wright wrote that "cigarette smoking and the danger to health which it poses are among the most controversial and important issues before the American public today." [1] Today, the controversy over the danger of cigarette smoking has morphed into many controversies over public smoking bans, suits against Big Tobacco, and First Amendment advertisement battles. The fierce debates sparked by the issue of smoking have not ended. If anything, they threaten to explode into a conflagration. The lawsuits against tobacco companies continue and will not likely abate in this era of toxic-tort litigation.

The U.S. Congress continues to introduce bills regularly that address tobacco and health. For example, Congress has introduced the following measures in recent years:

H.R. 3907 Stronger Tobacco Warning Labels to Save Lives Act—Introduced in March 2002, this bill would require more detailed labels addressing "diseases or fatal health conditions caused by cigarette smoking," "any physical addiction that results from cigarette smoking," "the influence that cigarette smoking by adults has on young children and teenagers," and "the health hazards of secondhand smoke from cigarettes." The bill would also require color graphics on warning labels showing a color picture of either a diseased lung, heart, or mouth or the negative impact of secondhand smoke.

HR 3047 The Tobacco Free Internet for Kids Act of 2003—Introduced in September 2003, this bill would prohibit the online or mail-order sale of tobacco products unless measures are taken to ensure that the buyer is not a minor.

S. 2626 The Youth Smoking Prevention and Public Health Protection Act—Introduced in June 2002, this measure would give the Food and Drug Administration jurisdiction to regulate tobacco as a drug. This bill would give Congress the authority to regulate cigarette marketing and advertising efforts and require larger warning labels.

Legislators continue to introduce bills requiring more explicit warning labels and giving the FDA authority to regulate tobacco products. But not all measures in the legislature target the tobacco industry as a villain. For instance, a resolution introduced in Congress by a senator from South Carolina (whose state makes enormous profits from tobacco crops) commended the tobacco company R.J. Reynolds for its past relationship with motor sports and stock-car racing.

Not only does the tobacco issue play a prominent role in the legislature, but the courts continue to hear cases filed against the tobacco industry and cases challenging smoking bans as well.

These cases involve issues of social and individual responsibility, expanded governmental power, tort reform, products liability, class-action lawsuits, and more.

The tobacco companies continue to make huge sums of money and spend millions upon millions aggressively marketing their products. Current cases will determine whether the tobacco companies have violated provisions of the Master Settlement Agreement, in particular the provisions against marketing to children. It also remains to be seen whether the tobacco giants will continue to abide by the Master Settlement Agreement.

The issue of the dangers of secondhand smoke will continue to rage as medical and scientific research continues to explore the effects of secondhand smoke. Will the movement toward limiting secondhand smoke lead to the banning of smoking in residential complexes? Will more parents lose child custody cases because of their smoking habits?

All of these questions confirm that smoking remains a burning issue in American society.

History of Tobacco and Its Regulation

1 *Lorillard Tobacco Co.* v. *Reilly,* 533 U.S. 525, 587 (2001), citing Amicus Brief for United States, p. 19.

2 Richard Kluger, *Ashes to Ashes.* New York: Alfred A. Knopf, 1996, p. 15.

3 Ibid., p. 16.

4 *Austin* v. *Tennessee,* 179 U.S. 343 (1900).

5 Ibid., p. 349.

6 Ibid., p. 362.

7 Kluger, p. 68.

8 Ibid., p. 109.

9 Philip J. Hilts, *SmokeScreen: The Truth Behind the Tobacco Industry Coverup.* Reading, MA: Addison-Wesley Publishing Company, Inc., 1996, p. 1.

10 Kluger, p. 114.

11 Ibid., p. 196.

12 Ibid., p. 205.

13 Ibid., p. 232.

14 Ibid., p. 242.

15 Ibid., p. 266.

16 Martin Redish, "First Amendment Theory and the Demise of the Commercial Speech Distinction: The Case of the Smoking Controversy," 24 N. Ky. L. Rev. 553, 579 (1997).

17 "Tobacco Industry Spent More Than $20 Million to Lobby Congress in 2002." Available online at *http://www.tobaccofreekids. org/Script/DisplayPressRelease.php3? Display=682.*

18 *FDA* v. *Brown & Williamson Tobacco Corp.,* 529 U.S. 120 (2000).

Point: Smoking Bans Protect Public Health

1 Available online at *http://www.jointogether. org/sa/news/summaries/reader/0,1854,56 7252,00.html.*

2 Del. Code Ann. 16 Section 2901-2908 (2001).

3 Rosemarie Henson et. al., "Clean Indoor Air: Where, Why and How," 30 J.L. Med. & Ethics 75, 77 (2002).

4 Cigarette Labeling and Advertising Act 15 U.S.C. 1333 (1965).

5 Peter D. Jacobsen, Jeffrey Wasserman, and John R. Anderson, "Historical Overview of Tobacco Legislation and Regulation," *Smoking: Who Has the Right?,* eds. Jeffrey A. Schaler and Magda E. Schaler. Amherst, NY: Prometheus Books, 1993, p. 47.

6 EPA, "Respiratory Health Effects of Passive Smoking." Available online at *http://www.epa.gov/ncea/ets/pdfs/ etsch1.pdf.*

7 Ibid.

8 National Cancer Institute, "Environmental Tobacco Smoke." Available online at *http://cis.nci.nih.gov/fact/ 3_9.htm.*

9 *Shimp* v. *New Jersey Bell Telephone Company,* 145 N.J. Super. 516, 526, 368 A.2d 408, 413 (1976).

10 Ibid., p. 416.

11 *Wilhelm* v. *CSX Transportation,* 2003 U.S. App. LEXIS 10864 (6th Cir.)(5/29/03).

12 *City of Tucson* v. *Grezaffi,* 200 Ariz. 130, 23 P.3d 675 (2001).

13 49 U.S.C. Section 41706.

14 *Nader* v. *Federal Aviation Administrator,* 440 F.2d 292, 294-295 (D.C. Cir. 1971).

15 Carrie-Anne Tondo, "When Parents Are On a Level Playing Field, Courts Cry Foul at Smoking," 40 Fam. Ct. Rev. 238, 246 (2002).

16 David B. Ezra, "'Get Your Ashes Out of My Living Room!': Controlling Tobacco Smoke In Multi-Unit Residential Housing," 54 Rutgers L. Rev. 135, 139 (2001).

17 *Helling* v. *McKinney,* 509 U.S. 25 (1993).

18 Ibid., p. 33.

19 *Brashear* v. *Simms,* 138 F.Supp.2d 693, 694 (2001).

Counterpoint: Smoking Bans Infringe on Smokers' Individual Rights

1 Robert W. Tracinski, "The Hazards of a Smoke-Free Environment," *CNSNews.com.* Available online at *http://www.cnsnews.com/Commentary/ Archive/200310/COM20031027d.html.*

2 Available online at *http://courses.albion.edu/ Archived_Summer2002/phil303/1115 SmokerFired.htm.*

3 Douglas J. Den Uyl, "Smoking, Human Liberties, and Civil Liberties," *Smoking: Who Has the Right?*, eds. Jeffrey A. Schaler and Magda E. Schaler. Amherst, NY: Prometheus Books, 1993, pp. 267–291.

4 Mark Edward Lender, "The New Prohibition." Available online at *http://www. brownandwilliamson.com/index_sub2.cf m?Page=/BWT/Index.cfm%3FID%3D98 %26Sect%3D4.*

5 "Multicenter case-control study of exposure to environmental tobacco smoke and lung cancer in Europe." Available online at *http://jncicancer spectrum.oupjournals.org/cgi/content/ abstract/jnci;90/19/1440?fulltext=^search id=QID_NOT_SET.*

6 Available online at *http://www.rjrt.com/ TI/TIHealth_Issues.asp.*

7 4 F.Supp.2d 435 (M.D. N.C. 1998).

8 Ibid., p. 463.

9 Ibid., p. 466.

10 *Flue-Cured Tobacco Cooperative Stabilization Corporation* v. *United States Environmental Protection Agency*, 313 F.3d 852, 862 (4th Cir. 2002).

11 D. Dowd Muska, "A Raw Deal for Secondhand Smoke," *Nevada Journal*, August 5, 1998. Available online at *http://www.npri.org/issues/issues98/ I_b080598.htm.*

12 Complaint at p. 11, n. 52.

13 *D.A.B.E., Inc.* v. *Toledo-Lucas County Bd. of Health*, 773 N.E.2d 536 (Ohio 2002).

14 Jason Hardin. "Rep. Altman files bill against smoking bans," *Charleston (S.C.) Post & Courier*, June 4, 2003.

15 *Loyal Order of Moose, Incorporated, Yarmouth Lodge #2270* v. *Board of Health of Yarmouth*, 790 N.E.2d 203 (2003).

16 Toby Coleman, "Power at center of court debate, Justices will decide if county smoking bans are legal," *Charleston Daily Mall* (West Virginia), October 8, 2003, p. 3C.

17 *Best Lock Corporation* v. *Review Board of the Indiana Department of Employment and Training Services*, 572 N.E.2d 520, 525 (1991).

Point: Suits Against Big Tobacco Are Legitimate Cases Against Wealthy Defendants Selling Harmful Products

1 Available online at *http://www.courttv.com/ archive/business/tobacco/1999/021199_ morris_ctv.html.*

2 Richard L. Cupp, Jr., "A Morality Play's Third Act: Revisiting Addiction, Fraud and Consumer Choice in 'Third Wave' Tobacco Litigation," 46 U. Kan. L. Rev. 465 (1998).

3 *Cipollone* v. *Liggett Group*, 505 U.S. 504, 509-510 (1992).

4 Ibid., pp. 524–525.

5 Ibid., p. 526.

6 George J. Annas, "Tobacco Litigation as Cancer Prevention: Dealing with the Devil," *Smoking Who Has the Right?*, eds. Jeffrey A. Schaler and Magda E. Schaler. Amherst, NY: Prometheus Books, 1998, p. 164.

7 *Castano* v. *American Tobacco Co.*, 84 F. 3d 734, 752 (5th Cir. 1996)

8 *Burton* v. *R.J. Reynolds Tobacco Company*, 205 F.Supp. 2d 1253, 1255 (D. Kan. 2002).

9 David Hechler, "Billions and Billions: Tobacco Takes It on the Chin," *National Law Journal*, February 3, 2003.

10 Howard M. Erichson, "The End of the Defendant Advantage," *Tobacco Litigation*, 26 Wm. & Mary Envtl. L. & Pol'y Rev. 123, 133–134 (2001).

Counterpoint: Suits Against Big Tobacco Ignore Personal Responsibility and Unfairly Demonize a Legal Activity

1 Available online at *http://www. smokingparadise.net/News/prohibition.html.*

2 Joseph L. Bast, "Smoking Under Siege: Why It Matters To You," September/ October 1997, Heartland Institute. Available online at *http://www.heartland. org/Article.cfm?artId=876.*

3 Jeffrey A. Schaler. "Smoking Right and Responsibility," *Smoking Who Has the Right?*, eds. Jeffrey A. Schaler and Magda E. Schaler. Amherst, NY: Prometheus Books, 1993, p. 333.

4 *Gibbs* v. *Republic Tobacco*, L.P., 119 F.Supp.2d 1288 (M.D. Fla. 2000).

5 *Roysdon* v. *R.J. Reynolds Tobacco Company*, 849 F.2d 230, 236 (6th Cir. 1988).

6 *Toole* v. *Brown & Williamson*, 980 F.Supp. 419 (N.D. Ala. 1997).

7 *Tompkins* v. *R.J. Reynolds Tobacco Company*, 92 F.Supp.2d 70, 89 (2000).

8 *Wajda* v. *R.J. Reynolds Tobacco Company*, 103 F.Supp.2d 29 (D. Mass. 2000).

9 *State Farm Mutual Auto Ins. Co.* v. *Campbell*, 123 S.Ct. 1513 (2003).

10 Ibid., p. 1524.

11 Available online at *http://www.supreme-courtus.gov/docket/02-1553.htm.*

12 Walter Williams, "Trashing the Rule of Law," *Capitalism Magazine*, October 7, 2003. Available online at *http://capmag.com/article.asp?ID=3155.*

13 John Alan Cohan. "Obesity, Public Policy, and Tort Claims," 12 Widener L.J. 103, 122 (2003).

Point: Advertising Restrictions Against Tobacco Products Help Protect Children and Are Constitutional

1 *Ohralik* v. *Ohio State Bar Ass'n*, 436 U.S. 447, 456 (1978).

2 Ibid., pp. 455–456.

3 *Virginia Pharmacy Board* v. *Virginia Consumer Council*, 425 U.S. at 772, n. 24.

4 *Central Hudson Gas & Elec. Corp.* v. *Public Serv. Comm'n of N.Y.*, 447 U.S. 557 (1980).

5 *Capital Broadcasting Company* v. *Mitchell*, 333 F.Supp. 582 (D.D.C. 1971).

6 Steve Allen and Bill Adler, *The Passionate Nonsmoker's Bill of Rights*. New York: William Morrow and Company, Inc., 1989, p. 29.

7 Yabo Lin, "Put a Rein on That Unruly Horse: Balancing the Freedom of Commercial Speech and the Protection of Children in Restricting Cigarette Billboard Advertising," 52 Wash. U.J. & Contemp. L. 307, 350 (1997).

8 *Clay* v. *American Tobacco Company*, 188 F.R.D. 483 (S.D. Ill. 1999).

9 Edward M. Kennedy, "The Need for FDA Regulation of Tobacco Products," 3 Yale J. Health Pol'y , L & Ethics 101, 103 (2002).

10 Charles King III and Michael Siegel, *The Master Settlement Agreement with the Tobacco Industry and Cigarette Advertising in Magazines.* Available online at *http://www.tobaccolaw.org/documents/english/literature/MasterSettlementAgreementwithTobaccoIndustryandCigaretteAdvertisinginMagazines.htm.*

11 American Heart Association, "Tobacco Industry's Targeting of Youth, Minorities and Women." Available online at *http://www.americanheart.org/presenter.jhtml?identifier=11226.*

12 Surgeon General's Report on Reducing Tobacco Use, "Tobacco Advertising and Promotion Fact Sheet." Available online at *http://www.cdc.gov/tobacco/sgr/sgr_2000/TobaccoAdvertising.pdf.*

13 Vernellia R. Randall, "Smoking, the African-American Community, and the Proposed National Tobacco Settlement." 29 U. Tol. L. Rev. 677 (1998).

14 Ibid., p. 682.

Counterpoint: Tobacco Advertising Is a Form of Protected Speech

1 425 U.S. 748 (1976).

2 *Capital Broadcasting Company* v. *Mitchell*, 333 F.Supp. 582, 587 (J. Wright, dissenting).

3 Ibid., p. 590.

4 *Rubin* v. *Coors Brewing Company*, 514 U.S. 476 (1995).

5 *44 Liquormart, Inc.* v. *Rhode Island*, 517 U.S. 484 (1996).

6 Ibid., p. 522 (J. Thomas, concurring).

7 15 U.S.C. 1334(b).

8 *Lorillard Tobacco Co. v. Reilly,* 533 U.S. 525, 587 (2001).

9 Ibid., p. 562.

10 Ibid., p. 564.

11 Ibid., p. 566.

12 David S. Modzeleski, "Lorillard Tobacco v. Reilly: Are We Protecting the Integrity of the First Amendment and the Commercial Free Speech Doctrine at the Risk of Harming Our Youth?" 51 Cath. U.L. Rev. 987, 1020–1021 (2002).

13 Michael Hoefges, "Protecting Tobacco Advertising Under the Commercial Speech Doctrine: The Constitutional Impact of Lorillard Tobacco Co.," 8 Comm. L. & Pol'y 267, 305 (2003).

14 David L. Hudson, Jr., "Tobacco Ads." First Amendment Center Online. Available online at *http://www. firstamendmentcenter.org/Speech/ advertising/topic.aspx?topic=tobacco_ alcohol.*

15 Margaret A. Little, "A Most Dangerous Indiscretion: The Legal, Economic, and Political Legacy of the Governments' Tobacco Litigation," 33 Conn. L. Rev. 1143, 1144 (2001).

Conclusion

1 *Capital Broadcasting Co. v. Mitchell,* 333 F.Supp. at 587 (J. Wright, dissenting).

Books and Articles

Allen, Steve, and Bill Adler, Jr. *The Passionate Nonsmoker's Bill of Rights.*
William Morrow and Company, 1989.
Antismoking book that discusses how to form nonsmoking advocacy groups,
how to draft nonsmoking legislation, and how to protect yourself from secondhand smoke.

Cohan, John Alan. "Obesity, Public Policy, and Tort Claims," 12 Widener
L.J. 103 (2003)
Law review article examines tort lawsuits against the fast-food industry and
compares them to suits against tobacco manufacturers.

Colb, Sherry L. "Smoking Bans in New York: Outrageous or Reasonable?
Findlaw.com, April 9, 2003. Available online at *http://writ.news.findlaw.com/
scripts/printer_friendly.pl?page=/colb/20030409.html.*
Well-written essay examining the smoking ban in New York City.

Cupp, Richard L., Jr. "A Morality Play's Third Act: Revisiting Addiction
Fraud and Consumer Choice in 'Third Wave' Tobacco Litigation," 46 U.
Kan. L. Rev. 465 (1998).
Informative law review article about the three waves of litigation against tobacco
manufacturers.

Erichson, Howard. "The End of the Defendant Advantage in Tobacco Litigation,"
26 Wm. & Mary Environmental Law and Policy Review 123 (2001).
Discusses how more recent suits against tobacco manufacturers are more successful
than earlier suits.

Ezra, David B. "'Get Your Ashes Out of My Living Room!': Controlling Tobacco
Smoke In Multi-Unit Residential Housing," 54 Rutgers L. Rev. 135, 139 (2001)
Law review article discussing issue of removing secondhand smoke from
residential areas.

Hechler, David. "Billions and Billions: Tobacco Takes It on the Chin,"
National Law Journal, February 3, 2003.
Legal newspaper article discussing large verdicts against tobacco industry.

Henson, Rosemarie, et al. "Clean Indoor Air: Where, Why and How,"
30 J.L. Med. & Ethics 75, 77 (2002)
Law review article discussing protection of clean-air and clean-indoor-air laws.

Hilts, Philip J. *SmokeScreen: The Truth Behind the Tobacco Industry Coverup.*
Addison-Wesley Publishing Company, Inc., 1996.
Book that blasts the tobacco industry's conduct in covering up the harmfulness
and addictiveness of its products.

Hoefges, Michael. "Protecting Tobacco Advertising Under the Commercial Speech Doctrine: The Constitutional Impact of *Lorillard Tobacco Co.*, 8 Comm. L. & Pol'y 267 (2003).
Law review article that discusses the *Lorillard* case and commercial free speech.

Kennedy, Edward. "The Need for FDA Regulation of Tobacco Products." 3 Yale J. Health Pol'y, L, & Ethics 101 (2002).
Short law review article discussing need for FDA regulation of tobacco products. Article talks about tobacco industry's relentless marketing to children even after the 1998 Master Settlement Agreement.

Kluger, Richard. *Ashes to Ashes.* Alfred A. Knopf, 1996.
Impressive, lengthy book examines history of tobacco regulation and tobacco companies' long history of less-than-admirable conduct.

Lin, Yabo. "Put a Rein on that Unruly Horse: Balancing The Freedom of Commercial Speech and the Protection of Children in Restricting Cigarette Billboard Advertising," 52 Wash. U.J. Urb. & Contemp. L. 307 (1997).
Law review article that discusses the issue of regulating tobacco billboards.

Little, Margaret. "A Most Dangerous Indiscretion: The Legal, Economic, and Political Legacy of the Governments' Tobacco Litigation," 33 Conn. L. Rev. 1143 (2001).
Comprehensive law review article explains why the Master Settlement Agreement was unconstitutional.

Luka, Lori Ann. "The Tobacco Industry and the First Amendment: An Analysis of the 1998 Master Settlement Agreement," 14 Clev. St. U. J.L. & Health 297.
This well-written law review article analyzes the constitutionality of the Master Settlement Agreement.

Modzeleksi, David S. "Lorillard Tobacco v. Reilly: Are we Protecting the Integrity of the First Amendment and the Commercial Speech Doctrine at the Risk of Harming Our Youth?" 51 Cath. U.L. Rev. 987 (2002).
Another law review article examining the *Lorillard* decision.

Randall, Vernellia R. "Smoking, the African-American Community, and the Proposed National Tobacco Settlement," 29 U. Tol. L. Rev. 677 (1998).
Article examines tobacco companies' history of targeting minorities in their advertising.

Redish, Martin. "First Amendment Theory and the Demise of the Commercial Speech Distinction: The Case of the Smoking Controversy," 24 N. Ky. L. Rev. 553 (1997).
Leading First Amendment theorist discusses commercial speech doctrine and the smoking controversy.

Schaler, Jeffrey A., and Magda E. Schaler, eds. *Smoking: Who Has the Right?* Prometheus Books, 1998.
This informative book contains a series of essays about the smoking controversy. Excellent resource because the book offers so many different perspectives. Highly recommended.

Schwartz, Allison D. "Environmental Tobacco Smoke and Its Effect on Children: Controlling Smoke in the Home," 20 B.C. Envtl. Aff. L. Rev. 135 (1993).
This law review article examines the effect of secondhand smoke on children and what can be done to protect them.

Shoop, Julie Gannon. "1999 Brings Up and Downs for Tobacco Plaintiffs," *Trial* (April 1999).

Tondo, Carrie-Anne. "When Parents Are On a Level Playing Field, Courts Cry Foul at Smoking," 40 Fam. Ct. Rev. 238, 246 (2002)
Law journal article discussing the issue of smoking in child-custody cases.

Websites

Americans for Non-smokers Rights

http://www.no-smoke.org/
This antismoking group provides good general information on issues relating to the smoking controversy.

Campaign for Tobacco Free Kids

http://www.tobaccofreekids.org/
This antismoking site contains lots of information about smoking issues.

Centers for Disease Control and Prevention

http://www.cdc.gov/health/tobacco.htm
This site contains information about harmful health effects of tobacco.

Federal Trade Commission

http://www.ftc.gov/os/2002/05/2002cigrpt.pdf
The Federal Trade Commission's Website has a lot of information about tobacco marketing, including a yearly report.

Forces Foundation

http://www.forces.org/index.htm
This prosmoking site takes issue with the antismoking campaign.

Master Settlement Agreement

http://www.tobacco.neu.edu/Extra/multistate_settlement.htm
This link provides the full text of the Master Settlement Agreement.

R.J. Reynolds Tobacco Company

http://www.rjrt.com/TI/TIsmokersRightsIssues.asp
This tobacco giant's Website has information on smoking litigation, cases, and underlying issues.

Smokers Club

http://www.smokersclub.com
This prosmoking site contains information about smokers' rights, including a newsletter.

Tobacco Control Resource Center, Inc. and the Tobacco Products Liability Project

http://www.tobacco.neu.edu/
This Website contains a wealth of information regarding tort cases filed against tobacco companies. It provides analysis of each case, with commentary from lawyers working with the groups. This site is highly recommended for anyone wishing to track tobacco litigation.

Tobaccodocuments.org

http://www.tobaccodocuments.org
This site contains documents from various tobacco companies.

Tobaccofree.org

http://www.tobaccofree.org
This site contains information urging people to quit smoking.

Tobacco.org

http://www.tobacco.org
This site contains much information on news about tobacco products, litigation, and more.

Case Law and Legislation

Austin v. Tennessee, 179 U.S. 343 (1900)
U.S. Supreme Court upholds Tennessee law restricting sale of cigarettes based on public health and safety and general police power of state.

Brashear v. Simms, 138 F.Supp.2d 693 (D. Md. 2001)
Federal district court rules against inmate who alleges that smoking is a disability under the Americans with Disabilities Act.

Burton v. R.J. Reynolds Tobacco Company, 205 F.Supp.2d 1253 (D.Kan. 2002)
Federal district court rules that smoker is entitled to recover punitive damages from tobacco company for its culpable conduct.

Capital Broadcasting Company v. Mitchell, 333 F.Supp. 582 (D.D.C. 1971)
Federal court upholds federal broadcast ban on cigarette advertisements.

Central Hudson Gas & Electric Corp. v. Public Serv. Comm'n of N.Y., 447 U.S. 557 (1980)
U.S. Supreme Court sets up four-part test to determine constitutionality of restrictions that impact on commercial speech.

D.A.R.E., Inc. v. Toledo-Lucas County Bd. of Health, 773 N.E.2d 536 (Ohio 2002)
Ohio supreme court rules that county health board lacked the authority to adopt clean indoor air, antismoking regulation.

Fagan v. Axelrod, 550 N.Y.S.2d 552 (N.Y. 1990)
New York court upholds state Clean Indoor Air Law.

Flue-Cured Tobacco Cooperative Stabilization Corporation v. United States Environmental Protection Agency, 4 F.Supp.2d 435 (M.D. N.C. 1998)
Federal judge questions validity of EPA study on harm of secondhand smoke.

Flue-Cured Tobacco Cooperative Stabilization Corporation v. United States Environmental Protection Agency, 313 F.3d 852 (4th Cir. 2002)
Federal appeals court reverses lower-court ruling on EPA study.

44 Liquormart, Inc. v. Rhode Island, 517 U.S. 484 (1996)
U.S. Supreme Court rules that Rhode Island laws banning alcohol price ads are unconstitutional; leading commercial speech case.

Gibbs v. Republic Tobacco, L.P., 119 F.Supp.2d 1288 (M.D. Fla. 2000)
Federal district court rules that loose-leaf tobacco is not an unreasonably dangerous product.

Goddard **v. *R.J. Reynolds Tobacco Company***, 75 P.3d 1075 (Ariz. 2003)
Arizona appeals court case dealing with tobacco company's alleged violation of
Master Settlement Agreement.

Guilbeault **v. *R.J. Reynolds Tobacco Company***, 84 F.Supp.2d 263 (D.R.I. 2000)
Federal district court rules that common-knowledge doctrine prevents plaintiffs'
products liability claim against tobacco company.

Helling **v. *McKinney***, 509 U.S. 25 (1993)
U.S. Supreme Court decision dealing with prisoner's lawsuit against prison
officials for failing to protect inmate from high levels of secondhand smoke.

Huddleston **v. *R.J. Reynolds Tobacco Company***, 66 F.Supp.2d 1370 (N.D.
Ga. 1999)
Federal district court rules that Georgia state law does not recognize claim for
intentional exposure to hazardous substance.

Liggett Group, Inc. **v. *Engle***, 853 So.2d 434 (Fla. 2003)
Florida Supreme Court rules that punitive damage award against tobacco
company is invalid in class-action suit.

Lorillard Tobacco Co. **v. *Reilly***, 533 U.S. 525 (2001)
U.S. Supreme Court decision on tobacco outdoor advertising; addresses both
First Amendment and preemption issues.

Loyal Order of Moose Incorporated, Yarmouth Lodge #2270 **v. *Board of
Health of Yarmouth***, 790 N.E.2d 203 (2003)
State high court rules that city smoking ban cannot be extended to private lodge.

Nader **v. *Federal Aviation Administration***, 440 F.2d 292 (D.C. Cir. 1971)
Federal appeals court rules against consumer advocate Ralph Nader in suit
advocating for smoking ban on air flights.

Roysdon **v. *R.J. Reynolds Tobacco Company***, 849 F.2d 230 (6th Cir. 1988)
Federal appeals court rules that tobacco cigarettes were not defective within
meaning of Tennessee products liability law.

Shimp **v. *New Jersey Bell Telephone Company***, 145 N.J. Super. 516, 368
A.2d 408 (1976)
New Jersey court decision holding that employer has duty to provide smoke-free,
safe environment for employee sensitive to secondhand smoke.

Soliman **v. *Philip Morris, Inc.***, 311 F.3d 966 (9th Cir. 2002)
Federal appeals court rules that smoker loses on fraudulent concealment claim
against tobacco company.

Tompkins **v. *R.J. Reynolds Tobacco Company***, 92 F.Supp.2d 70 (N.D.N.Y. 2000)
Federal district court rules that tobacco manufacturer is not liable on express
warrant claim and had no duty to disclose.

Toole v. *Brown & Williamson Tobacco Corporation*, 980 F.Supp. 419 (N.D. Ala. 1997)
Federal district court rules that tobacco cigarettes were not an unreasonably dangerous product within the meaning of Alabama's products liability law.

Virginia State Bd. of Pharmacy v. *Virginia Citizens Consumer Council, Inc.*, 425 U.S. 748 (1976)
U.S. Supreme Court landmark ruling on commercial speech.

Wajda v. *R.J. Reynolds Tobacco Company*, 103 F.Supp.2d 29 (D.Mass. 2000)
Federal district court rules that tobacco company cannot be civilly liable under the RICO (Racketeer Influenced and Corrupt Organizations) Act.

Waterhouse v. *R.J. Reynolds Tobacco Company*, 270 F.Supp.2d 678 (D. Md. 2003)
Federal district court ruling barring fraudulent concealment claim against tobacco company. Court also rules that plaintiffs' civil conspiracy claim can move forward.

Terms and Concepts

causation
commercial speech
comparative negligence
contributory negligence
due process
First Amendment
negligence
preemption
products liability
punitive damages
secondhand smoke
statute
tort

Beginning Legal Research

The goal of POINT/COUNTERPOINT is not only to provide the reader with an introduction to a controversial issue affecting society, but also to encourage the reader to explore the issue more fully. This appendix, then, is meant to serve as a guide to the reader in researching the current state of the law as well as exploring some of the public-policy arguments as to why existing laws should be changed or new laws are needed.

Like many types of research, legal research has become much faster and more accessible with the invention of the Internet. This appendix discusses some of the best starting points, but of course "surfing the Net" will uncover endless additional sources of information—some more reliable than others. Some important sources of law are not yet available on the Internet, but these can generally be found at the larger public and university libraries. Librarians usually are happy to point patrons in the right direction.

The most important source of law in the United States is the Constitution. Originally enacted in 1787, the Constitution outlines the structure of our federal government and sets limits on the types of laws that the federal government and state governments can pass. Through the centuries, a number of amendments have been added to or changed in the Constitution, most notably the first ten amendments, known collectively as the Bill of Rights, which guarantee important civil liberties. Each state also has its own constitution, many of which are similar to the U.S. Constitution. It is important to be familiar with the U.S. Constitution because so many of our laws are affected by its requirements. State constitutions often provide protections of individual rights that are even stronger than those set forth in the U.S. Constitution.

Within the guidelines of the U.S. Constitution, Congress—both the House of Representatives and the Senate—passes bills that are either vetoed or signed into law by the President. After the passage of the law, it becomes part of the United States Code, which is the official compilation of federal laws. The state legislatures use a similar process, in which bills become law when signed by the state's governor. Each state has its own official set of laws, some of which are published by the state and some of which are published by commercial publishers. The U.S. Code and the state codes are an important source of legal research; generally, legislators make efforts to make the language of the law as clear as possible.

However, reading the text of a federal or state law generally provides only part of the picture. In the American system of government, after the legislature passes laws and the executive (U.S. President or state governor) signs them, it is up to the judicial branch of the government, the court system, to interpret the laws and decide whether they violate any provision of the Constitution. At the state level, each state's supreme court has the ultimate authority in determining what a law means and whether or not it violates the state constitution. However, the federal courts—headed by the U.S. Supreme Court—can review state laws and court decisions to determine whether they violate federal laws or the U.S. Constitution. For example, a state court may find that a particular criminal law is valid under the state's constitution, but a federal court may then review the state court's decision and determine that the law is invalid under the U.S. Constitution.

It is important, then, to read court decisions when doing legal research. The Constitution uses language that is intentionally very general—for example, prohibiting "unreasonable searches and seizures" by the police—and court cases often provide more guidance. For example, the U.S. Supreme Court's 2001 decision in *Kyllo* v. *United States* held that scanning the outside of a person's house using a heat sensor to determine whether the person is growing marijuana is unreasonable—*if* it is done without a search warrant secured from a judge. Supreme Court decisions provide the most definitive explanation of the law of the land, and it is therefore important to include these in research. Often, when the Supreme Court has not decided a case on a particular issue, a decision by a federal appeals court or a state supreme court can provide guidance; but just as laws and constitutions can vary from state to state, so can federal courts be split on a particular interpretation of federal law or the U.S. Constitution. For example, federal appeals courts in Louisiana and California may reach opposite conclusions in similar cases.

Lawyers and courts refer to statutes and court decisions through a formal system of citations. Use of these citations reveals which court made the decision (or which legislature passed the statute) and when and enables the reader to locate the statute or court case quickly in a law library. For example, the legendary Supreme Court case *Brown* v. *Board of Education* has the legal citation 347 U.S. 483 (1954). At a law library, this 1954 decision can be found on page 483 of volume 347 of the U.S. Reports, the official collection of the Supreme Court's decisions. Citations can also be helpful in locating court cases on the Internet.

Understanding the current state of the law leads only to a partial understanding of the issues covered by the POINT/COUNTERPOINT series. For a fuller understanding of the issues, it is necessary to look at public-policy arguments that the current state of the law is not adequately addressing the issue. Many groups lobby for new legislation or changes to existing legislation; the National Rifle Association (NRA), for example, lobbies Congress and the state legislatures constantly to make existing gun control laws less restrictive and not to pass additional laws. The NRA and other groups dedicated to various causes might also intervene in pending court cases: a group such as Planned Parenthood might file a brief *amicus curiae* (as "a friend of the court")—called an "amicus brief"—in a lawsuit that could affect abortion rights. Interest groups also use the media to influence public opinion, issuing press releases and frequently appearing in interviews on news programs and talk shows. The books in POINT/COUNTERPOINT list some of the interest groups that are active in the issue at hand, but in each case there are countless other groups working at the local, state, and national levels. It is important to read everything with a critical eye, for sometimes interest groups present information in a way that can be read only to their advantage. The informed reader must always look for bias.

Finding sources of legal information on the Internet is relatively simple thanks to "portal" sites such as FindLaw (*www.findlaw.com*), which provides access to a variety of constitutions, statutes, court opinions, law review articles, news articles, and other resources—including all Supreme Court decisions issued since 1893. Other useful sources of information include the U.S. Government Printing Office (*www.gpo.gov*), which contains a complete copy of the U.S. Code, and the Library of Congress's THOMAS system (*thomas.loc.gov*), which offers access to bills pending before Congress as well as recently passed laws. Of course, the Internet changes every second of every day, so it is best to do some independent searching. Most cases, studies, and opinions that are cited or referred to in public debate can be found online—and *everything* can be found in one library or another.

The Internet can provide a basic understanding of most important legal issues, but not all sources can be found there. To find some documents it is necessary to visit the law library of a university or a public law library; some cities have public law libraries, and many library systems keep legal documents at the main branch. On the following page are some common citation forms.

COMMON CITATION FORMS

Source of Law	Sample Citation	Notes
U.S. Supreme Court	*Employment Division* v. *Smith*, 485 U.S. 660 (1988)	The U.S. Reports is the official record of Supreme Court decisions. There is also an unofficial Supreme Court ("S.Ct.") reporter.
U.S. Court of Appeals	*United States* v. *Lambert*, 695 F.2d 536 (11th Cir.1983)	Appellate cases appear in the Federal Reporter, designated by "F." The 11th Circuit has jurisdiction in Alabama, Florida, and Georgia.
U.S. District Court	*Carillon Importers, Ltd.* v. *Frank Pesce Group, Inc.*, 913 F.Supp. 1559 (S.D.Fla.1996)	Federal trial-level decisions are reported in the Federal Supplement ("F.Supp."). Some states have multiple federal districts; this case originated in the Southern District of Florida.
U.S. Code	Thomas Jefferson Commemoration Commission Act, 36 U.S.C., §149 (2002)	Sometimes the popular names of legislation—names with which the public may be familiar—are included with the U.S. Code citation.
State Supreme Court	*Sterling* v. *Cupp*, 290 Ore. 611, 614, 625 P.2d 123, 126 (1981)	The Oregon Supreme Court decision is reported in both the state's reporter and the Pacific regional reporter.
State statute	Pennsylvania Abortion Control Act of 1982, 18 Pa. Cons. Stat. 3203-3220 (1990)	States use many different citation formats for their statutes.

DAVID L. HUDSON, JR., is a research attorney with the First Amendment Center in Nashville, Tennessee. He also serves as a First Amendment contributing editor for the American Bar Association's *PREVIEW of United States Supreme Court Cases.* He obtained his undergraduate degree from Duke University and his law degree from Vanderbilt University School of Law. This is his sixth book.

ALAN MARZILLI, of Durham, North Carolina, is an independent consultant working on several ongoing projects for state and federal government agencies and nonprofit organizations. He has spoken about mental health issues in more than twenty-five states, the District of Columbia, and Puerto Rico; his work includes training mental health administrators, nonprofit management and staff, and people with mental illness and their family members on a wide variety of topics, including effective advocacy, community-based mental health services, and housing. He has written several handbooks and training curricula that are used nationally. He managed statewide and national mental health advocacy programs and worked for several public interest lobbying organizations in Washington, D.C., while studying law at Georgetown University.